Careers in Journalism for the New Woman

Careers in Journalism for the New Woman

by Megan Rosenfeld

Series Editor: Mary Louise Birmingham

CHOOSING CAREERS and LIFE-STYLES

Franklin Watts/New York/London/1977

Library of Congress Cataloging in Publication Data

Rosenfeld, Megan.
    Careers in journalism for the new woman.

    (Choosing careers and life-styles)
    Bibliography: p.
    Includes index.
    SUMMARY: Discusses journalism as a career with atten-
tion to preparation needed, schools, types of jobs on various
publications, and women in American journalism.
    1. Journalism — Vocation guidance — Juvenile literature.
2. Women in journalism — Juvenile literature.
[1. Journalism — Vocational guidance. 2. Women in journalism. 3. Vocational guidance] I. Title.
PN4797.R6   070'.023   76-43362

ISBN 0-531-00371-X

Contents

1

An Introduction, 1

2

Preparing for Journalism, 7

3

Journalism Schools and Majors, 16

4

Dailies, Wire Services, Newsmagazines, 23

5

Broadcast Journalism, 40

6

Trade Journals and Other Publications, 53

7

Free-Lance Writing, 64

8

Public Relations, Public Information, and
Government Jobs, 69

9

Women in American Journalism, 81

10

Job-Hunting, 87

11

Conclusion, 96

Appendix: Schools and Departments of Journalism, 101
Bibliography, 109
Index, 111

Careers in Journalism for the New Woman

1

An Introduction

In 1971 a young woman was hired by a large metropolitan daily newspaper as a city staff reporter. For
weeks she was assigned stories about education or religion, and although she had experience covering hard
news she was never sent out on a breaking story—a still-
unfolding surprise event.

She had a master's degree in journalism from a prestigious school, four years' experience working on a large
campus newspaper, and had spent two years writing for
a wire service. Nonetheless, her editors had avoided
every chance to send her out on "the street," giving her
instead "safe" stories that did not require meeting a
daily deadline.

One day, at lunchtime, the city editor got a call that
two women had been raped that morning in two downtown office buildings. The reporter watched as her
editor searched the newsroom, looking for a male reporter to send out on the story. They were all out to
lunch. He had no choice but to send her.

She turned in the story, well before deadline, and

watched as some of the more graphic details of the rape were edited out. At last the editor looked up and said, with an unmistakable tone of surprise: "Hmmm, this isn't bad!"

Today that woman is in the editor's chair. She has three times as many women on her staff as her editor did, and she has no qualms about sending them out on a breaking news story, no matter how grisly.

Until fairly recently, women were considered freaks in the news business. Those who were hired were generally assigned to the women's page, where they covered food, fashion, social events, and other topics that male editors thought needed a "woman's touch."

The few women who did cover news, whether it was a crime story, a trial, or a war, were exceptions rather than the rule. But today, opportunities for women in journalism are growing rapidly, just as in society as a whole we are adjusting our ideas of a "woman's role."

Now there are women covering the White House (the President, not the First Lady), Congress, the Supreme Court, Wall Street, and national as well as local politics. There are women foreign correspondents, sportswriters, and editorial writers. Even the traditionally female fields—food, fashion, and so forth—are being covered with more professionalism than ever, as reporters branch into consumerism as opposed to faddism.

In many cities there are women in the radio and television field, anchorpersons, women reporters, and even a few producers and news directors. In the field of public information, women are being given more responsibility and better jobs.

In 1920, according to U.S. Census figures, there were 5,730 women "reporters and editors." In 1930 there were 11,924. By 1960 there were 39,001 and in 1970, 61,478.

The number of women admitted to journalism schools between 1964 and 1974 increased by 295.2 percent, according to a survey of juniors and seniors by *Journalism Educator* magazine, although the same survey showed that women's proportion of the total enrollment has stayed at about 40 percent during the last seven years.

Although men still outnumber women by the thousands—especially in the upper echelon jobs—these numbers are nevertheless encouraging. They tell us that the field of journalism is opening up to women, and, as in other traditionally male occupations, progress has been made toward acceptance of the idea that a person should be hired for ability and not gender.

Journalism is a not a profession for anyone who wants a "normal" life. The hours are long and unpredictable. There is no routine. Salaries start, on the average, at $140 or $150 a week. Good health, both mental and physical, is essential—especially that elusive quality known as a "thick skin."

Journalism is a profession marked by tension. The pressures of meeting deadlines, of having people slam a door in your face because they don't want to talk to you, of probing into people's lives will inevitably affect your life.

They are pressures you should consider carefully, because if you can't deal with them you will be unhappy in journalism. It is impossible not to care when an editor or someone you're trying to interview yells at you. It is impossible not to be affected by witnessing human tragedy or corruption. But it is possible to learn how to deal with these feelings, how to retain your sense of humor and perspective. The stereotype of the calloused journalist, seemingly impervious to human emotions, has a grain of truth to it. But more and more journalists are finding that it is possible to have feelings and still make your deadline.

There is no well-defined way to prepare for journalism as there is for professions such as law or medicine. Every woman interviewed for this book got her job through a different route. Some were college dropouts (not recommended) and some had master's degrees in journalism. Some worked on small papers before getting a job at a bigger one, others started on a wire service, and others began their careers as lowly copy aides.

They have degrees in political science, art, history, theater, English, French, and philosophy. Some got their first job quickly because they knew someone; others had to apply for thirty or forty jobs before they found an opening.

Some women have husbands and children and are successful in combining family life with their careers—usually with the help of a housekeeper. Others are single and like it that way. A few women, who have decided they want to stay at home while their children are young, are able to make a living by free-lancing.

Two editors on the city desk of the Washington *Post* are good examples of different routes to a top job on a leading newspaper.

Judy Luce Mann, who recently had her second child and is married to a free-lance writer, is a college dropout. In high school she worked on the school paper and had a part-time job on a local paper, which she got with the help of her best friend's mother. As a "teen" correspondent, she filed news about her high school and had the opportunity to watch the operations of a weekly newspaper. In college she majored in political science and was involved in student government activities. She didn't plan for a career in journalism, but there came a time when she needed a job and found one with "the only skill I had"—writing. She got a job writing summaries of books for a book review digest.

Responding to a newspaper advertisement, she applied for a job as the assistant editor of a weekly paper in northern Virginia. This job led to one at the now-defunct Washington *Daily News,* where she was both an editor and a writer. When the *News* folded, Judy was one of the few people hired from that paper by the *Post.*

Karlyn Barker, who has the job of assistant city editor, put out her first newspaper at the age of eight and hasn't stopped working since. She edited her junior high school paper, her high school paper, her junior college paper, and her college paper—in her case, *The Daily Californian* at the University of California at Berkeley, which had at the time a circulation of 65,000.

She majored in English and minored in journalism but spent most of her time working on *The Daily Cal.* After graduation, she got a job as a dictationist at United Press International, taking down stories phoned in by reporters. She left UPI to get a master's degree from Columbia University's Graduate School of Journalism in New York City, then returned to UPI as a reporter. After almost a year at UPI, she quit, wanting to leave New York, and applied for a job at the Washington *Post.* After four years as a reporter, she is learning the job of an editor.

The jobs available within the field are almost as varied as the ways to prepare yourself for them.

A journalist might be an editor, a copy editor, a film

editor, a public information specialist, a public relations executive, or a television producer as well as a reporter. You might work for a daily or weekly newspaper, a newsmagazine, a wire service, a special interest magazine, or a government agency.

You might work at a small radio station or at home, writing free-lance articles. You might work for a paper with a specific political viewpoint or one aimed at a special audience. You might work for a school system or for a police department as a public information officer, responsible for collecting information about that organization for the press.

The common denominator in each of these jobs is: news. Whether or not a journalist is operating under a daily deadline, the raw material of a reporter or editor's job is what's-happening-now. It is, perhaps, this attraction to the immediate, this fascination with the urgency of current events, that sets a journalist apart from those in other professions.

A young woman television reporter, successful, attractive, and professional, was discussing her experience of friendships with men who were not journalists. A few months earlier she had decided to stop going out with other journalists, because she felt isolated and wanted to meet people in other worlds.

"I just wanted to spend an evening with a man who didn't flinch every time fifteen fire engines went by," she said. "So I started seeing stockbrokers and lawyers and we went to a lot of nice restaurants, and they didn't flinch at fire engines.

"But it didn't work out. First of all, I found most of them boring. And the other thing was—they couldn't understand why *I* flinched every time fifteen fire engines went by."

2

Preparing for Journalism

The debate over whether a journalist should go to a journalism school has been going on since the first schools were founded in 1905.

In such fields as medicine, law, or social work, a degree in the field is a prerequisite. A degree in journalism is not a must for getting a job as a journalist. There are many routes to a job, and many opinions as to which is the most productive and practical.

If you are still in high school, there are two ways you can give yourself a head start: keep abreast of current events and learn as much as you can about the English language. The latter is particularly important. Language will be the basic tool of your career. A thorough working knowledge of its structure is essential. Concentrate on spelling and grammar, and learn to write simple, clear prose.

Read a newspaper every day. Study the stories that have caught your attention. Why are they interesting? Why were others not? Compare the way a newspaper handles a particular story with the way it's done on television. Absorb the news, so that it becomes part of your general knowledge.

And a typing course never hurt anyone.

Many high schools are now offering introductory courses in journalism. Taking one of these can be a good way to begin, particularly if you also work on the high school newspaper. Representatives of 2,500 high school publications belong to the National Scholastic Press Association, an organization that holds workshops and conferences for high school journalists.

A beginning course usually includes field trips to local newspapers or broadcast facilities, an introduction to the history of journalism, and the basics of news writing, along with some instruction on libel laws. At Langley High School in Virginia, for example, one journalism class functions as the school's "press bureau," giving students an opportunity to write press releases about school events that are distributed to other schools and local newspapers. In some schools, where the equipment is available, students produce news programs on closed circuit television. A high school course in journalism can be an excellent way of tasting and testing the life of a journalist.

In 1974 enrollment in journalism schools reached an all-time high—55,078 students, an increase of 13.8 percent over 1973, according to a survey by Dr. Paul Peterson of Ohio State University. Average enrollment in other disciplines increased by only 4 percent during the same period.

In 1974 12,125 journalism degrees were awarded. The Newspaper Fund, a nonprofit organization devoted to attracting young people to careers in journalism, surveyed about half of them (6,561) and found that fewer journalism graduates were finding jobs in the field than in 1973. Less than half, about 44 percent, found jobs at newspapers, wire services, radio or television stations, magazines or other media. Another 18.5 percent went into advertising or public relations. The rest found jobs in teaching, went into graduate school or military service, or into an unrelated field. Some—8.9 percent—were unemployed.

Of those who did get jobs, however, 43.3 percent were women.

What these numbers tell us, if anything, is that a degree in journalism is no guarantee of a job. In another survey of 185 daily newspapers, the Newspaper Fund learned that of the people hired by these papers in 1974, 42 percent were hired directly from college and three-fourths of these people were journalism majors or minors.

One woman who recently got a job at a major newspaper said that her first contact with journalism was as a summer intern at a small paper. At the end of the summer the editors at the paper told her she should get a graduate degree in journalism, that without any journalism courses on her record they couldn't hire her. So she went back to school and got the degree. When she started applying for jobs after graduation, she was told repeatedly by prospective employers, "We aren't interested in degrees; we're more interested in experience."

Every employer wants someone who is talented, trained, experienced, reliable, responsible, and cooperative. They want people who are well-educated and have a wide range of skills and information. Curiosity, initiative—these wonderful qualities are also valued in journalism.

There are those who feel that the best way to develop these attributes is by getting the best possible liberal arts education and practical experience by writing at every opportunity. There are editors who think that journalism school limits a young person and teaches unnecessary habits.

Some journalists complain that "J-School" rarely teaches the student anything practical, that writing in a classroom situation bears so little resemblance to a deadline situation that it is a futile exercise, and the student would be better off learning history or economics. A large part of being a good journalist, they say, is common sense—and you can't teach that.

On the other hand, some professionals say that journalism school gives the beginner a chance to learn the basics of the craft in an environment that fosters professionalism and a knowledge of the ethics and standard practices of journalism. A good school, with a range of facilities, gives a young person a chance to experiment with different media, to try out television or radio or magazine writing. Having successfully completed a course, the young job-seeker can present at least one recognizable credential to a prospective employer.

The Newspaper Fund puts out a useful booklet, *A Newspaper Career and You* (P.O. Box 300, Princeton, N.J. 08540). In it, Professor M. L. Stein of the Journalism Department at the University of California at Long Beach writes:

The major comes away with a knowledge of the history and tradition of his profession. He learns something about news media problems, their relationships to society and government, and their function in a democracy. He is informed about the communication process, and is presented with an ethical basis for his actions. Above all, he is made aware of his responsibilities as a journalist.

Another view holds that a graduate degree in a field other than journalism, such as economics or law, is a great advantage. This type of credential is especially appealing to the larger newspapers and newsmagazines. Coupled with practical experience on another newspaper, a college paper, or another job that required writing skills and the ability to meet a deadline, the person with a graduate degree may edge out other applicants.

Linda Mathews, for example, was hired to cover the Supreme Court for the Los Angeles *Times* when she was twenty-five. She had worked as a high school sports stringer for the paper before going to Radcliffe College. There, she majored in government and worked for three years on the Harvard *Crimson,* first as a reporter and copy editor and later as managing editor. After she graduated in 1967, she got a job at the Los Angeles *Times*—after writing them a letter saying she wouldn't cover women's news and she wouldn't be a copy aide.

"I think I lucked out," she said. "At the time, the paper had one woman in the newsroom, and she'd had to spend twelve years in the women's section before getting out. I think they were looking for women and I happened along at the right time."

After two years as a general assignment reporter in Los Angeles, Linda returned to Harvard to go to law school. She worked for the Washington bureau of the L.A. *Times* during the summer, and when she graduated was offered the job of covering the Supreme Court.

"I'm sure that the law degree is what made them hire a twenty-five-year-old for the job," she said. "Although sometimes I think my editors are more convinced than I am of the effectiveness of a law degree. My colleagues without one seem to manage very well, but I think my editors think it is quite a coup."

Linda is married to Jay Mathews, a reporter on a major metropolitan daily who also worked on the *Crimson*. Later, he did graduate work in Far East Asian studies, specializing in Chinese. After several years on the suburban staff of the *Post*, Jay is assigned to the coveted Hong Kong bureau, undoubtedly a result of his graduate specialty in addition to his reportorial skills. Linda will join him in Hong Kong after the next session of the Supreme Court is over. She expects to have lined up a job there by then.

The Mathewses have a young son, who is looked after four days a week by a housekeeper. Linda and Jay share only one day off together, so Jay takes care of the child on Fridays and Linda is with him on Sundays.

"It works out well," Linda said. "I'm there in the mornings and at night. Our baby-sitter is flexible if, because of one crisis or another, we have to work late."

Working on a college newspaper can be a most productive way to learn the craft. There are 1,900 college newspapers in the country, according to a directory compiled by Dario Politello of the University of Massachusetts. Of these, 640 publish weekly and 117 publish more than four times a week. The total circulation of college newspapers is estimated at 2,241,000 on any given day.

On some campuses the newspaper functions as the town newspaper as well. The Columbia *Daily Missourian*, published at the University of Missouri, is the major paper in the town of Columbia. The Cornell *Daily Sun* is an important paper in Ithaca, N.Y. Large campus newspapers, those with substantial staffs, budgets, and circulations, tend to be found at large schools and universities. Some of them are published entirely by students, others are affiliated with departments of journalism.

Linda Mathews said her work on the Harvard *Crimson* was the only journalistic training as such that she received in school. There were no courses in the field available. To get on the *Crimson* staff was a competitive business. Older editors and reporters on the staff taught the younger ones.

The Daily Californian at Berkeley now has a circulation of 22,000 and a budget of $400,000. It has offices off-campus, and 98 percent of its funding comes from advertising revenues, according to 1975 managing editor Jeffrey Rabin. The paper is distributed free.

The university itself pays $8,000 for its 2,500 annual subscriptions, Rabin said, but contributes no other funds. The paper is not affiliated with the university's School of Journalism.

The Daily Cal is run by a senior editorial board of nine; in the fall of 1975 three of those people were women. There were fourteen staff reporters, of whom eight were women, and ten copy editors, including five women. The staff changes every six months.

Everyone on the staff is paid, from $60 a month for a reporter to $275 a month for the editor-in-chief. Each staff reporter is expected to turn in one or two stories a week. The paper publishes five days a week during the school year and twice weekly during the summer.

Rabin said *The Daily Cal* has a larger circulation than Berkeley's city newspaper. For this reason the student paper covers the city council, the school board, and other citywide concerns as well as campus news. It covers student government and puts out a weekly arts section. It does not publicize things like dances, however, preferring to "emphasize news," he said. Recent stories include investigative pieces on the university's affirmative action program and the influence of Iranian donations to the school. The paper also publishes a summary of national and international news, a weekly consumer column directed at college students, and a food page. Issues run from twelve to thirty-two pages.

He estimated that only half of the staff members were journalism majors. Fewer still wanted to go into journalism professionally.

Karlyn Barker started working as a reporter on *The Daily Cal* in 1966. She remembers her first front-page story for the paper, a week after she had volunteered to be on the staff:

I was assigned to cover a meeting of student activists who were planning an anti-war rally. Jerry Rubin was there and said that he envisioned 10,000 students marching on the chancellor's office. I had enough sense to know this was a good story, but I couldn't believe it when I called the office and my editor said he wanted it for the next day's paper! It was ten o'clock at night and somehow it was supposed to be on the street in the morning. It was my first experience with a deadline. If it hadn't been for the editor's help with the story, I don't know what I would have done. But it was down the tube at midnight. I was so excited I stayed around until the edition came out, although I knew I'd probably be locked out of my dorm.

Another reporter interviewed for this book was a theater major in college. She wanted to be an actress and went to New York City after graduation with the hope of breaking into show business. After discovering she didn't like New York and finding it nearly impossible to get a job, she moved back to her hometown and, "through luck and the fact that my father knew the editor of the section," got a job as an assistant in the arts and society section of a local newspaper.

One day when there were no other reporters available, she was asked to review a play. She did, and discovered she enjoyed writing. She began suggesting story ideas and writing the stories on her own time. After two years of writing about the arts, she applied for a summer internship on the city news section of the paper, and was accepted. This program led to another internship, also on the city desk. Her successful performance as an intern led eventually to a position as full-time staff reporter.

Preparing for a career in journalism is obviously a confusing prospect. Somehow you will want to combine experience with training in specific skills and a broad general education. You will want to be exposed to different types of media so that you can decide which area to aim for.

Do you want to work at a small paper, where you will have a direct personal relationship with your employers and your community, or do you prefer a competitive urban setting? Do you want to write in-depth, analytical pieces or crank out breaking news on a deadline? Or both? Do you see yourself behind a microphone or at an editor's desk? What about publishing your own newspaper? Do you want to be a specialist in one field or cover everything that your editor decides is worth covering?

You may be able to answer these questions after a few years in school, whether or not you major in journalism. On the other hand, you may not know what you really want to do until you have working experience in the field.

3

Journalism Schools and Majors

If you decide to major in journalism in college, you will have at least 192 departments and schools of journalism to choose from, according to a list in the January 1975 edition of *Journalism Educator.*

These range from departments with two or three persons on the faculty to places like the University of Missouri, which boasts a school of journalism with a staff of seventy-one, curricula in advertising, newsmagazine journalism, broadcasting, publishing, and photojournalism, and facilities that include a campus radio and television station, a darkroom, and access to all the major wire services.

Before choosing a school, it is important to investigate its facilities. Of these schools, 176 have some sort of radio or television facility, ranging from a campus-run radio station to access to local commercial stations. Some 120-odd schools are on campuses where a campus newspaper is published independently of the department but used in the academic program. Twenty-one schools have a newspaper produced by the journalism department in addition to a campus newspaper.

Find out if the school has any internship programs with commercial media outlets. An internship is a learning apprenticeship. These jobs can be extremely valuable, paid or unpaid. Examine the school newspaper for its quality. Find out whether beginners are supervised and helped or left to develop news-gathering skills on their own. If you are interested in writing for magazines, find out if one is published on campus.

Look at the credentials of the faculty to discover their specialities. If you are interested in broadcasting you probably should not choose a school where most of the teachers come from print media backgrounds. Faculty members with regular jobs on a newspaper or magazine or in broadcasting can sometimes be helpful when the time comes to look for a job.

Consider the location of the school. A school in a large city offers the advantage of access to local media and the people who work at them. In a smaller town, however, the campus newspaper may be of vital importance to the area. It may therefore offer opportunities to cover city councils and politics that another student paper wouldn't bother with.

The American Council on Education for Journalism (ACEJ), a group authorized by the National Commission on Accrediting to accredit journalism schools, recommends that only one-fourth of a major's undergraduate courses be in journalism and that these courses should be concentrated in the last two years of a four-year course.

To get the broad and liberal education you need in college, you will choose most of your freshman-sophomore courses and about half of your junior-senior courses from such fields as anthropology, economics, esthetics, history, literature, management, marketing, philosophy, political science, psychology, sociology, speech, and other arts and sciences.

The liberal education will provide the base for your professional education in journalism and a career which requires great energy and a strong sense of responsibility, but offers most satisfactory rewards. You may agree that the combination of professional journalism and liberal arts and sciences is superior to a straight liberal arts program. It has been a common experience that students with a professional education in journalism not only start with a distinct advantage over students without that specialized training, they stay well ahead of them.

These passages are from a booklet called *Education for a Journalism Career* published by the ACEJ. (Single copies are available at no cost from the ACEJ, c/o the School of Journalism, University of Missouri, Columbia, Mo. 65201.) This booklet, which is rather boring and not very informative, does include a list of the 61 journalism schools the ACEJ has accredited.

A survey of 140 schools of journalism and communications showed that the three most frequently offered undergraduate courses are Reporting I, Introduction to Journalism/Mass Communications, and Radio-TV-Film. The other most frequently offered courses are: Photojournalism, Reporting II, Advertising, Mass Communication Theory, Public Relations, Mass Communication Law, and Editing II. Other courses include Editing I, Specialized Writing and Reporting, Mass Communication History, Graphic Arts, and Publications Practice Lab.

This survey was done by Nanci Knopf Dawdy, who teaches at Mohave High School in Mohave, California.

Other courses listed by the Newspaper Fund in "A Newspaper Career and You" are: history of journalism, literature of journalism, grammar for journalists, press law and ethics, newspaper economics and management, and journalism research.

Schools that allow students to devise interdisciplinary courses on their own provide an excellent opportunity for a journalism student. Combining, for example, sociology and the role of the media in society might be fruitful, or writing a magazine piece for a literature course to fulfill a term paper requirement.

More than $2 million in scholarship aid is available to journalism students. Most, however, is restricted to special kinds of applicants. Little is specifically earmarked for women, unless they are members of minority groups.

There are forty graduate programs in journalism accredited by the ACEJ. These programs, generally more intense and more complex than a four-year program, result in a master's degree on successful completion of the program and a master's thesis, which usually requires a year.

Lyssa Waters graduated from the Graduate School of Journalism at Columbia University, one of the most prestigious programs in the country, in 1975. She described her first assignment for Reporting and Writing I, a requirement in the first semester.

There was a note in my mailbox that said "Something is going on at Lincoln Hospital in the South Bronx. Find out what that is and how the community feels about it." This was a Wednesday morning and I was supposed to have the story in by Thursday night. I knew enough about New York City to know that the South Bronx was a rough neighborhood. Sure enough, when I got lost and asked for directions, the man who helped me said "Lady, you'd better get out of here." This was at nine o'clock in the morning!

I located the hospital, which had been threatened with loss of accreditation for poor sanitary conditions. They were struggling to clean it up, because it was the only hospital in the area.

When I got there I found out that a young doctor who ran a controversial detoxification center for drug addicts had been murdered the day before. He was found with a needle in his arm, though everyone said he was definitely not an addict. This doctor had just received a grant to experiment with acupuncture to help drug addicts.

I called my teacher and said, "This doctor has been murdered, what do I do?!" He answered, "Go back and find out everything you can about it." The New York *Daily News* and the New York *Post* had already been there. No one wanted to talk to the press. I was standing in the detox center trying to talk to an attendant. Suddenly these two guys who looked like thugs started coming at me. I ran down the hospital corridors until I found a policeman. The two "thugs" turned out to be security guards assigned to keep the press out of the center.

By that time I'd had it. I told my teacher I was leaving the hospital and I was going to do the rest of the story by phone. He was furious and told me I'd never make it as a journalist. Later this same teacher said he would make me cry before the semester was over.

Lyssa completed the semester without crying. She decided to specialize in magazine writing, particularly in the science field. She credits the course with giving her confidence, practice, and knowledge of what it takes to cope with the real world.

"We found out that it was unwise to unburden yourself to a teacher, except for a few. They didn't want to know about your private agonies—it embarrassed them. I suspect that this is true at a large newspaper or magazine, so in a sense it was a good thing to learn."

Lyssa and another 1975 graduate, Gretchen Keiser, described a year of study that was busy and intense. "You don't get to see your friends much," Lyssa said, "and you think it's wonderful if you get a chance to wash your clothes."

For the first semester, the week began with a 9 A.M. "press conference." A public figure or authority on some problem would be invited to give a talk. Students were expected to question him and write a story based on the session within an hour or two after it was over.

On Monday afternoon Lyssa had a seminar on ethics. The evenings were usually spent on homework and outside reading. For the first seven weeks of the term she had an editing class three hours a week. She learned to write headlines, lay out a newspaper page, and edit wire service copy. During the second seven weeks of the term, these three hours were devoted to a session on broadcast journalism. She learned to film, write, and edit a small TV documentary as well as to produce, write, and report for radio broadcasts.

As an elective, Lyssa took an evening class taught by anthropologist Margaret Mead, which involved outside reading. At least two full days were taken up with the Reporting and Writing I course. Each week she had an assignment such as the one at Lincoln Hospital, as well as one investigative piece and a profile once during the term.

A magazine seminar took up another three or four hours a week. Gretchen spent this time in a course on suburban writing, where she learned to write the type of stories she might be doing if she worked for the local desk of a newspaper.

Friday morning was devoted to a class in libel laws. On top of everything else, the first draft of a master's thesis was due the day after the end of Christmas vacation.

"Sometimes I think I learned as much from the other students as I did from the courses," Gretchen said.

If you choose to go to journalism school, one situation you will not have to endure is that described by Ishbel Ross in her 1936 book, *Ladies of the Press.* She reported that in 1926 Professor Charles P. Cooper set up a separate copy desk for women at Columbia's Graduate School of Journalism. The women had to produce a newspaper with a four o'clock deadline. They had to produce the entire paper, from writing headlines and editing copy to making up pages. The idea was to test the women to see if they were as competent as the male students.

Surprise! They were.

4

Dailies, Wire Services, Newsmagazines

It was a rainy Sunday morning, and the reporter was looking forward to a leisurely day off at home. At 11 A.M. the phone rang.

"Listen," her editor said, without an apology for the disruption. "A plane with ninety-seven people on board just crashed into a mountain because of the rainstorm. We understand there are no survivors. The relatives of the victims are presumably waiting at the airport where the plane would have landed if it hadn't crashed. Go over there and find some relatives, and see if you can find out who was on the plane."

"Okay," she said.

"Swell," she thought. "Instead of a pleasant day at home, I've got a day driving around in the rain asking people how they feel about their mothers being killed in a plane crash."

Ten hours later, after working nonstop all day, calling in every hour to dictate information about the victims, their families, and the confusion at the airport created by the rainstorm and the crash, she thought she might be allowed to go home.

"Listen," another editor said when she called in asking to be relieved. "We hear the rain has caused bad flooding in the area. Drive up and down the parkway and see if the water is covering the road."

"You want me to drive into a flood?" she asked.

"Oh come on, you can always turn back if it gets too deep," he said. "But be sure to call us."

Two hours later she was allowed to go home. Damp and too tired to be hungry, she fell asleep knowing she'd be spending the next day on follow-up stories about the plane crash and the weather.

The public image of a journalist is usually the hard-news reporter or editor. Although the profession encompasses a wide variety of jobs, the common denominator is the reporter on the street, racing to make the next deadline.

Whatever kind of journalism is your final choice, there is no substitute for daily news experience. Many eminent newspaper or television columnists and critics, authors of books or magazine articles, public spokespersons or press secretaries, and even publishers started their careers working the police beat for a daily newspaper or covering a state legislature for a wire service. Even those who end up as playwrights, poets, screenwriters, or novelists frequently put in a few years in the news business.

Daily news-gathering demands speed, common sense, the ability to organize facts, persistence, and, above all, a commitment to accuracy. It can mean hours of boring work as well as the exciting pressure of a breaking story such as the plane crash.

Even within the field of daily news there is a spectrum

of occupations and styles. Writing for a newsmagazine is very different from writing for a wire service, and copy editing demands skills a reporter doesn't use.

The style of writing varies greatly from one publication to another as well, and a journalist may find an affinity for one paper, while she can't dream of working for another. Here are three leads (first paragraphs) from New York newspapers on the same story, appearing in the August 18, 1975, editions:

The New York Times:
Samuel Bronfman 2d, the 21-year-old heir to the Seagram liquor fortune, was rescued at 4 A.M. yesterday on the ninth day of his kidnapping. He was freed without violence by 40 to 60 Federal Bureau of Investigation agents and New York City policemen who surprised a captor in an apartment in the Flatbush section of Brooklyn.

The *Daily News:*
Samuel Bronfman, kidnaped heir to a billion-dollar whisky fortune, was rescued yesterday by police and FBI agents who arrested two alleged kidnapers—a city fireman and a limousine service operator—and recovered the $2.3 million cash ransom paid 24 hours earlier.

The *Post:*
The sensational kidnapping of Seagram's heir Samuel Bronfman 2d, which seemed last week like a highly sophisticated crime, turned out to be the apparent work of two men whose amateurish mistakes led to their easy capture.

Notice, aside from the differences in information, the stylistic variations. *The New York Times* says "Federal Bureau of Investigation," while the *Daily News* uses the abbreviation "FBI."

Going further into the stories, we can find an example

of another peculiarity of hard news. According to the *Daily News*, Bronfman's first words on being rescued were "Thank God you're here." Then, they reported, he called his father and said: " 'Dad, I'm okay,' Sam said. 'Thank you.' "

According to *The New York Times*, Bronfman's first words were "Thank God." His first words to his father, the *Times* reported—attributing the report to "police rescuers"—were "Dad, I'm all right. Thanks for everything, Dad."

In the *Post*, Bronfman said "Thank God, thank God." when rescued, and then "where am I." When he reached his father, he reportedly said "Dad, I'm okay. I'm all right. I'm safe. Thank you." The *Post* attributed the report to a detective.

Which newspaper was accurate? Probably all of them. But this relatively minor example illustrates some of the subtleties of reporting and editing. Each paper probably got the quotes from a different source, none of whom may have actually been in the room when Bronfman was rescued and called his father. The writers of each story chose to include different quotes—or their editors may have cut the quotes they did include. They agreed only in reporting that Bronfman said "Thank God" and thanked his father.

There are some working differences among newspapers, newsmagazines, and wire services that are worth discussing.

Newspapers

There are 1,819 daily newspapers in the United States and 8,824 weeklies. Jobs on them are in great demand, no matter how small the paper is. Since the Washington *Post* took over the Trenton *Times* in the fall of 1974, for example, the paper has received more than 2,500 applications for jobs on a newsroom staff of 100. The Chicago *Sun Times* gets more than 700 applications a year from people just out of school—that's about two a day.

The editorial staff of a newspaper (as distinct from advertising or production people) generally includes reporters, editors, copy editors, makeup editors, photographers, research assistants or librarians, and copy aides (formerly known as "copyboys"). The smaller the paper, the fewer the employees, naturally, and the greater the likelihood that one or more of these jobs is done by the same person.

On a paper large enough to have both assignment and copy editors the functions are different. The assignment editor, as the title indicates, assigns reporters or approves assignments suggested by reporters and is responsible for coordinating their work and for deciding whether a story is worth a reporter's time. The assignment editor also acts as copy editor on smaller publications and reads the story written by the reporter and edits it for style, organization, grammar, and spelling.

The assignment editor also checks the story for libel. The editor may ask the reporter for more facts or for a rewrite. Depending on the personnel structure within a particular newspaper, this editor may also decide the importance of a story and where it should go in the newspaper. If assigned to a particular section of the paper, such as the city desk or the sports section, the editor is also responsible for keeping an overview of the coverage, making sure that important stories are followed up and trends spotted. The editor must also be able to trim the story beyond the first edited version, if it is longer than the space (newshole) allotted, without changing the meaning of the story.

Copy editors are experts in grammar, spelling, and the style of the newspaper. They also write the headlines for stories—a difficult job to do well. Copy editors also have direct contact with the composing room, where the copy is set in type.

A makeup editor designs the page, choosing and placing pictures and juggling the number of stories on the page. Every page has the same amount of space, but the number of stories and how much of the story will appear on the page is determined by type size and other visual factors. For example, if the editor wants a large picture on the page, a story may have to be moved elsewhere.

Adrienne Cook was a copy editor for the St. Petersburg *Times* and later for the Annapolis *Evening Capital*. At the *Times* she worked on the "A" desk, which handled national news for the paper, and was also responsible for makeup:

> Every paper is different. At the *Times* we had about eight wire services to provide national news. Our first job was to read all versions of a particular story and then decide which parts of which stories we wanted. Then we'd piece them all together into one story.
>
> Occasionally you'd have a story with a local angle and you'd insert copy from a *Times* reporter. But mostly we dealt with these wire stories. Each editor had about six inside pages to lay out—the head of the copy desk did Page One.

The layout of a page is called a dummy. The first task of a layout editor is to find out how much of the page is taken up by advertising—the remaining space is called the newshole. Then the editor finds out how many stories have to fit on that page. At the *Times,* Adrienne said:

You first decide which story is the most important and then lead with that story. If you have a page with very little advertising on it, you want to have a picture to make the page more readable. So you decide how large the picture should be and mark that. Then you start reading and editing the stories—you can't decide which one is the lead story until you've read it—and writing headlines and captions for the pictures. As you finish each page you draw up the dummy, writing the slug (name) of each story and the first few words of the headline in the appropriate place on the dummy and send it down to the composing room. After dinner we'd go to the composing room to make sure it was being done right.

The *Times* had a newsroom staff of about 140. At a larger paper, the jobs of layout and copy editing would be done by separate people. At a smaller paper—such as the *Evening Capitol,* which had a staff of 25—the editor would have even more responsibility.

"At the *Capitol* we had to do a lot of rewriting and dealt directly with reporters," Adrienne said. "I felt the work was more creative at the smaller paper, although I didn't have much time to experiment with layout because there was so much to do."

Adrienne, who now writes a weekly shopping column for the Trenton *Times,* says that copy editing attracts the kind of person who has a feel for the language and for the way a paper looks. "A copy editor doesn't get much ego gratification," she said. "But you can really enjoy taking a bad story and making it better by finding the holes in it and filling in the points that are missing. I'm concerned about the way the paper looks—that's my real love—and I think it's important. It's your job to make the reader want to read the story. You contribute greatly to the quality of the paper."

The worst part of the job, she said, is correcting proofs. "I think every copy editor hates that part."

The copydesk is often a place for a young person starting out or an older person on the way out. It is unfortunate that few journalists see the work as anything but a way station, because there are opportunities for being creative on the desk. But, as Adrienne said, "it's not a glamour job."

Research assistants and librarians are found on papers that can afford them. Their primary job is to find the stories on a particular subject that the paper has published before in the library, sometimes called The Morgue. A good newspaper has a system of clipping and filling each day's product so that stories are easily retrievable. Researchers also go beyond the paper's library to get statistics and facts from other published sources.

Copy aides are the lowest on the newspaper totem pole. However, if there were to be a convention of all the former copy aides in the country, some of the most famous and respected journalists, politicians, lawyers, and writers would show up. Most copy aides are young people curious about newspapering and working their way up. The job may be part drudgery and part fun, but it can give you invaluable knowledge of how a newspaper functions.

The original function of the "copyboy" was to carry the pages of a reporter's story to the editor as they came out of the typewriter. Copyboys also sharpened pencils, fetched coffee, and carried proofs from the composing room to the copydesk.

These days copy aides are rarely expected to sharpen

pencils, fetch coffee, or carry "hot" copy. Reporters and editors can do that themselves. Aides still carry proofs, however, and they also answer the telephone—a very important job at a newspaper—and may be asked to type lists of weddings and engagements, crimes, or the weather.

Reporters, as we know, gather facts. Usually they write the stories as well—the days of phoning in facts to a "re-write" person are pretty well over. In cases of emergency several reporters may be assigned to cover various angles of a particular story, while another reporter co-ordinates their reports into one piece.

If the newspaper is large enough, a reporter may be assigned to a particular "beat." On a small newspaper, with only two or three reporters, everyone covers everything. Generally, the larger the paper, the greater the number of beats.

Some beats—such as city hall, the White House, or education—are specific. Being assigned to one of these beats makes the reporter responsible for everything that happens in that area. If another newspaper scoops a story, the reporter covering that beat is usually the one who gets yelled at. Some reporters cover one beat for so many years that they become experts in the field.

Other beats are unofficial. There may be one reporter, with expertise in a particular field who is called upon whenever a story turns up in that field. If you speak French, know how to sail, or have some other special skill, you might be called when the skill is needed.

Other reporters are classified general assignment. That means doing anything and everything—from murders to parties to political campaigns. Some reporters prefer the variety of general assignment. Others are frustrated by never having time to know a field thoroughly.

Whatever your job on a newspaper, one element is omnipresent: the Deadline. Although each newspaper's deadline is different, generally an afternoon paper "closes" sometime between 8 A.M. and noon, and a morning paper between 6 P.M. and midnight.

In any case, the importance of the deadline cannot be overemphasized. You cannot miss your deadline. If you do, the story won't get into the paper and you won't have your job for very long. The production of a newspaper is a complex chain of events. The type can't be set until the story is in the composing room. The pages can't be made up until the type is set. The presses can't be started until the pages are in place. The newspaper can't be assembled until the pages are printed. After the newspaper has been printed, it has to be bundled, distributed to deliverers, and driven to different locations where it is picked up by a paper carrier.

A weekly newspaper's deadline is usually the day before it is published. However, since most weekly newspapers have small staffs, one reporter may be writing two or three stories for one edition. Thus, the days before the deadline may be more leisurely than on a daily, but the twenty-four hours or so before publication are punishing.

When Judy Luce Mann edited a weekly paper in northern Virginia, she put out seven editions once a week with a staff of three. She did everything—writing and reporting stories, designing layout, writing headlines—and the two days before the paper came out she would have to leave her baby son with her mother because she knew she wouldn't be home much.

Young reporters and editors often have dreams—or nightmares—about not being able to meet the deadline.

They dream they are stuck in traffic or unable to find a telephone.

"Once I dreamed I was caught in a mob of people," said one reporter. "I guess I was covering a demonstration or something. There was a big clock on a tower and I could see the hands of the clock moving toward six. The more I struggled to get out of the crowd, the more they struggled to push me back. I don't remember the end of the dream. I guess I made it somehow."

Wire Services

There are two main wire services in the United States, the Associated Press (AP) and United Press International (UPI). Both are vast news-gathering networks, with correspondents or stringers (a reporter called on occasionally who is not a full-time employee) in almost every area in the world. The wire services operate around the clock and almost every newspaper, magazine, and radio and television station that covers news subscribes to one service or both. The AP or UPI Teletype receiver—which clacks away constantly—is a standard feature everywhere.

Wire services differ from other media in two important ways—the style of writing and the deadline. Wire services are in constant competition to file a breaking story first—even if it's only a difference of minutes—so when something happens they flash a "bulletin" even if it's just a paragraph. Sometimes these bulletins— President Kennedy has been shot or New York City has narrowly avoided bankruptcy—are immediately read on the air by a radio announcer.

Both AP and UPI have an "A" or national wire and a

"B" or local area wire. The day is divided into two 12-hour periods, AM and PM. One period is geared for morning newspaper deadlines and the other for afternoon papers.

The wire service style is even more simple and direct than most newspaper writing, because the service is being used by so many different newpapers. Sometimes a newspaper editor will take the idea from a wire service story and assign a local reporter to get the story in more detail. At other times an editor will combine AP and UPI reports with local staff work and use the credit line "from news dispatches and staff reports."

Wire services, which also provide pictures and feature stories, are often asked by a member paper to cover a story of particular interest to that paper. Most newspapers pride themselves on using few wire stories, depending more on original reporting by their own staff. There is no question, however, that the wires are a vitally important source of information to any news organization.

Peg Simpson covers the House of Representatives for the Associated Press. She is one of a staff of five. Before her assignment to the House staff, she covered several Congressional delegations, writing stories geared for publication in a delegate's home state.

Before getting her coveted Washington assignment, Peg worked in Texas bureaus for the AP. For a time she was a copy editor in Dallas, working a shift from 3:30 P.M. to midnight or from 10:30 P.M. to 7 A.M.

"I didn't mind the night shifts because so few people were around then that you were in charge of the whole operation. But I was always falling asleep. . . . At the time there was actually a law in Texas that said women couldn't work after midnight unless the employer paid their cab fare home."

Peg covered the legislature in Austin and spent more time editing. About two years after she'd started working for AP, she asked a supervisor about the possibility of her eventually becoming a bureau chief.

"He laughed and said it wouldn't work because you had to go to publishers' meetings and drink men under the table," she remembered. "But that is the only specific example of overt sex discrimination I can recall. In a wire service, everybody has a hard time."

Karlyn Barker was a dictationist for UPI after graduating from college. A dictationist sits at a typewriter wearing a headset of earphones. Reporters call in and dictate breaking stories to the dictationist. She types them directly onto copy paper, which is ripped out sheet by sheet by an editor anxious to move the story. These days, dictationists also type onto computer terminals, which look like a combination of a television screen and a typewriter.

Karlyn was paid $92.50 a week. The experience was valuable, she said, because she could observe reporters and how they worked, but after a while it was frustrating. She thought of a story idea for the religion editor, who liked it. Eventually she was writing pieces for him regularly. She left to go to graduate school and was hired as a reporter in New York after she got her degree.

Once Karlyn was sent to cover a fire.

It was in a skyscraper and people couldn't get out of the building. Several people had died. I called my desk and reported that four people had been killed. My editor said "AP is reporting three," so I had to check it out. The scene was so confusing—you'd get one answer from one fireman and a different one from another. But I saw the ambulance carrying the bodies

hadn't left yet—there was only way way to really be
sure. I went over to the ambulance, looked in, and
counted the bodies. There were four. I'd never seen a
dead body before, but I was too worried about getting
the story right to feel squeamish.

There are other news services providing copy for
groups of client newspapers. Some services specialize in
covering the federal government, for example, for papers
that can't afford their own Washington correspondent.

Other services cater to special interests. The College
Press Service, in Denver, Colorado, for example, sends
stories to college papers of particular interest to students
and syndicates cartoons from member papers. The
American Indian Press Association advertises itself as a
"news service to American Indians."

Whatever the service, the basic jobs of reporter and
editor remain relatively similar to those functions on a
newspaper.

Newsmagazines

Working for a national newsmagazine—*Time, Newsweek, U.S. News & World Report*—is vastly different from
working on a newspaper or for a wire service.

The two major newsmagazines have bureaus or correspondents in every major city. They also have "back of
the book" departments—theater, business, press, and so
on. Although assigned to a bureau, a beat, or a department, a reporter may also be called on to get information
for any story in the magazine.

Unlike their counterparts on newspapers or wire services, newsmagazine reporters do not write their own
stories. They write "files," which are used by a writer as

the basis for the story. The story may then be rewritten by an editor.

Sometimes the writer is using files from many correspondents throughout the country, and at other times from only one reporter. The pace of a newsmagazine is slightly more relaxed than that of a daily newspaper. While a magazine writer may work on one or two stories a week, a newspaper reporter is usually expected to write a story daily.

As a result, the newsmagazine story can aim for more depth than a newspaper story generally provides. Although a story may actually be shorter than the newspaper versions, the magazine usually tries to put the story in historical context, discuss its impact, or report on similar events in other cities.

Researchers are vital to newsmagazines. They are low on the totem pole, but the job is important. For years this was the best job a woman could get on a newsmagazine. Researchers provide reporters and writers with background on a particular story or search out specifically requested pieces of information. Then they double-check facts in the story and read back the final version to the reporter to make sure that nothing has been misinterpreted.

Occasionally the researcher prepares a supplementary box of information. When President Ford was almost shot in California in 1975, both *Time* and *Newsweek* printed a list of previous assassination attempts on chief executives. The list ran separately from the main story in a ruled-off box.

The assembly-line structure of a newsmagazine creates inevitable conflict. "Sometimes you file something you know is terrific, really well-written," said

Phyllis Malamud, who has been a reporter for *Newsweek* for ten years. "When you see what the writer does to it, it breaks your heart. A newsmagazine is no place for anyone with a fragile ego.

"Newsmagazine journalism is really a factory. Sometimes we call it 'blender journalism.' Generally a writer has more status than a reporter, and an editor has more than a writer."

Phyllis was a history major in college, and after graduation got a job in the publicity department at *Newsweek*. At the time she had no thoughts of being a journalist, but found she liked the atmosphere of the office. Her first responsibility was answering Letters to the Editor. When the business department needed a researcher, she applied for the job and got it. Later she moved on to become chief researcher in other departments. After a few years she was one of the first women promoted to being a reporter.

"Being a researcher is definitely a gateway to becoming a reporter," she said. "The problem now is that researchers seem to lack ambition and respect for their own job. It is a low status job, but there are some departments where a researcher gets more chances to do real reporting than in others. It's the only job here you can get without any previous experience."

Consider all the types of work available in daily news writing before you decide on one in particular. Experience in more than one area is always an advantage. Some reporters start as copy editors; others do it the other way around. An editor's responsibilities and pressures are different from those of a reporter, and the best reporters are conscious of them. Reporters like to complain about their editors, and the editors are always griping about their reporters. Usually the complaints stem from a lack of understanding of another person's job.

The frustrations and rewards of each job vary, and you may find your temperament more suited to one than another. "I hated going around asking people personal questions," said one former reporter who is now an editor. "I always felt that I was being too nosy."

A reporter felt differently. "I couldn't stand being stuck at a desk," she said, "I like being out on the street where things are happening."

5

Broadcast Journalism

Although a generation of Americans has grown up with round-the-clock radio and television, broadcast journalism is still relatively new—and the field is still changing rapidly.

One of the recent advances in broadcast journalism is greater opportunities for women, including women from minority groups. Barbara Walters may be the only female anchorperson on the national networks, but many local stations have women anchoring or co-anchoring their news programs, and women reporters are starting to appear on the screen or the air regularly.

Broadcast journalism is the most powerful form of journalism. It reaches more people than any other medium, but air-time is so costly and the nature of communication such that television and radio news tends to touch only the story being reported. For context, depth, background, or complexity, people generally turn to newspapers or magazines.

The field has tremendous advantages in covering major breaking news stories. Reporters on the scene can relay news almost as soon as it happens. Some types of story, particularly those whose primary impact is visual, can be handled better by television than by any print media. If a building is described as being in terrible condition, for example, it can be more effective to show this condition than to write long paragraphs about the cracked plaster and leaky roof.

Time is to a broadcast journalist what space is to a newspaper person. The brevity of television and radio stories is a source of frustration as well as one of the medium's great advantages. Consider that a long television story would be three or four minutes—and most stories are only seconds long.

Time—immediacy—is the broadcast journalist's greatest advantage as well as greatest enemy. A television or radio news broadcast must deal with things that are happening now, today, not last week or the day before. A print journalist can reconstruct an event after it has happened if necessary. A television reporter must be there on the scene or there won't be any film to make the story.

Broadcast journalists are still refining their profession. Some are trained news people with expertise in electronic media. Others are former announcers or show business veterans who know only how to make a story "punchy" and interesting. Some reporters are hired for their expertise, others for their looks, their skin color, or their sex appeal. There is a high turnover in announcers, reporters, and anchorpersons in the broadcast field, particularly in television.

There is continual debate among broadcast journalists— particularly women—about whether people are hired for their good looks and mellifluous voice or for their journalistic skill. Since women have only recently been accepted as reporters, few of them have been around long enough to know whether they will be fired as soon as they start getting wrinkles and gray hair. They worry about it.

"You don't have to be beautiful," said one associate television producer who has known many women television journalists. "But you have to have a special quality. So and So comes across like the Girl Next Door, another woman has sex appeal, and the third has a sort of smart-ass quality. The fourth reporter here has basically no quality at all, and she isn't going to last long."

There is no question that television and radio reporters have to cultivate their personal appearance and use their voices well. Clear diction is essential in both fields, and a well-modulated, pleasant voice usually helps.

"Let's face it, this business is as much entertainment as it is journalism," said the same associate producer. "Some of the reporters like to think of themselves as serious journalists—and some of them are—but it's the personalities that draw the audience, and all the company cares about is ratings and making money."

There are 721 commercial television stations now licensed by the Federal Communications Commission. There are 4,357 AM radio stations, 2,448 FM radio stations, and 771 educational radio stations. Most of these stations, in order to keep their licenses, do some form of news and public affairs programming. Some radio stations are now using a twenty-four-hour-a-day, all-news format, utilizing teams of twenty or more reporters as well as wire services and network "feeds." Others are small-time stations where the news is delivered by an announcer who "rips and reads" the latest copy off the AP or UPI Teletype.

The production of a news program for radio or television is very different from the production of a newspaper. Even a small television station will have a producer, perhaps an assistant, a film editor, a camera operator, and an announcer or a newscaster. (An announcer delivers everything from dog food commercials to program changes; a newscaster is involved strictly with news.)

Larger television stations have associate producers, who work with reporters in a relationship somewhat similar to an editor's with a newspaper reporter. There are also research assistants, graphics experts, technicians, and writers.

The jobs related to journalism are those of reporter, newscaster, producer, and writer.

To illustrate briefly the difference between television, radio, and newspaper writing, read these three versions of the same story:

The radio version:

Outside Buenos Aires, Argentina, this morning, five policemen assigned to the unit that guards President Isabel Peron's palace were shot and killed by urban guerrillas. The policemen were ambushed with machine gun fire and hand grenades just after they got off work. Mrs. Peron was not anywhere near the policemen when they were killed.

The newspaper version:

BUENOS AIRES—Some 15 terrorists ambushed two carloads of police on their way home from guard duty at President Isabel Peron's residence yesterday, killed five of them and seriously wounded a sixth, authorities announced. The ambush occurred three miles north of Peron's home. She was spending the weekend at a resort 250 miles south of Buenos Aires.

Witnesses said a station wagon crashed into one of the police cars, while two other cars hemmed in the other police vehicle. The gunmen jumped out of the cars and opened fire with submachine guns and grenades while other terrorists fired at the police from the tops of nearby buildings.

The television version:

An ambush by terrorists left five policemen dead in Buenos Aires today. The shootings occurred near Argentina's presidential palace.

Before you decide to become a broadcast journalist, consider carefully the differences between television and radio. Although they are both "electronic journalism," their demands differ. You may be suited for one but totally unfit for the other.

Most reporters in both mediums are general assignment. There are few beat reporters in broadcast journalism, because not that many reporters are hired. Even if there were, there wouldn't be enough time to get all of their stories on the air. All reporters must therefore keep well-informed about local, national, and international events by reading newspapers and magazines.

Radio

When Betsy Ashton went to apply for her first full-time job as a radio reporter, the first thing the news director asked her to do was write a five-minute newscast from a stack of "A" wire copy. He gave her twenty minutes to do it, then recorded it.

She got the job, and for $9,000 a year became the first woman member of a staff of nine reporters. She worked from 5 A.M. to 2 P.M., covering all kinds of news.

Betsy quickly learned to tape and edit interviews, to write her stories in simple, direct sentences, and to speak into a microphone. She also learned one of the basic things about radio: there is a continual deadline.

Most radio stations have a newscast at least once an hour; some every half hour. Network affiliates may do their own program of local news on the half hour and a network newscast on the hour. This means that stories are changed and updated during the day as things happen. The 10 A.M. broadcast may bear no resemblance to the 2 P.M. broadcast. The morning story may be an announcement—the President has scheduled a press conference—which is replaced by the story when it actually happens.

Radio reporters must learn to use tape recorders. Sometimes the reporter covers an event—say a press conference—and has time to go back to the office, write a story summarizing what was said, edit the tape for an appropriate quote, and consult with the newscaster about a "lead-in" to her story.

At other times interviews are taped over the phone, a story is written by hand in a phone booth, and the story dictated over the phone into a machine at the radio station. A taped interview can be transmitted over the telephone with a special "loop."

After a year and half at the smaller radio station, Betsy was offered a job with a larger station at almost twice the salary.

"I learned a lot about production at [the smaller station]," she said. "But at the new station I had a beat. The staff was larger—twenty-three reporters—and much more professional."

She now has a job as a television reporter—one of the few to make the switch from radio. "In radio you have to hustle more," she said. "Because of the deadlines. In TV you're working for only two deadlines."

Betsy does not have a degree in journalism. She feels that the technical aspects of radio and television can be learned quickly outside a school. She thinks it more important for a young woman to get "as good an education as possible at a good school." She sang in a choir during high school and this taught her vocal control and modulation, she said.

Other reporters recommend experience with the campus radio station. Not everyone is as self-confident as Betsy. "Mike fright" can be alleviated by experience. It takes a person with nerves of steel not to panic when a tape breaks or when the engineer puts on a commercial instead of a correspondent's story. A radio reporter must have the ability to handle such a disaster as well as the daily hustle of instant street reporting.

A radio newscaster is usually responsible for writing the whole newscast. Using wire services, newspapers, and correspondents' reports, the newscaster decides which news to report, how much to include and when, and then writes the script—usually with the assistance or approval of a producer or news director.

Much of the beauty of radio lies in its simplicity. Armed with a tape recorder and a note pad, a radio reporter can get important information to the public quickly and directly. The audience learns to depend on certain radio stations for news about the weather and traffic before they leave for work and about office and school closings on holidays or in the event of a natural disaster. In some areas of the world, the radio is a lifeline to the rest of the world.

Television is not so simple.

Television

The newsroom of a television station looks much like that of a small newspaper. Groups of desks with tele-

phones and typewriters for the reporters, a bank of writers at another side of the room, phones ringing, Teletype machines clicking. But look closer. One of the
first things you'll notice is that the type on the typewriters prints out large capitals, which are easier to read.

The staff begins preparing for the six o'clock news by
9:30 in the morning. Reporters are dispatched on assignments with camera crews, the newspapers are read
for important stories that should be picked up, and cal-
endars are checked for other important events.

A half-hour news program must be interesting as well
as informative. Some stations try especially to entertain,
with comic meteorologists or zany movie reviewers or
stories done on horseback or on a roller coaster to spice
things up. There is an effort to avoid the overuse of
"talking heads"—that is, reporters or newscasters just
sitting there and reading copy. "Visuals"—slides, graphs,
maps—are used whenever possible if there is no film to
go with the story. It is a demanding task to coordinate news stories, sports news, the weather, and feature
stories with their respective film clips and visuals as
well as commercials into a half-hour newscast.

A television reporter must think about what to film as
well as what to say. Besides getting the facts, she must
decide what will be interesting on film. Action shots of
people doing something are better than a talking head,
but the story cannot always be told this way. TV reporters complain that they never have enough time to develop innovative film ideas.

It's hard for a TV reporter to be unobtrusive. Trailed
by a three-man camera crew with lights, sound equipment, rolls of extra film and cables, the TV reporter's
very presence changes the event she is trying to cover. In-
terviewees may be reluctant to appear on camera or may

turn shy and mumble. Children jump up and down behind the person being interviewed, trying to get into the picture.

"Sometimes kids make the film unusable," said Linda Ellerbee, a television reporter who has worked in Houston and New York. "It says something about the power of television that they are so intent on getting into the picture."

Linda Ellerbee got her first television job at a small network affiliate in Houston, Texas. She had no TV experience but had reported for a wire service. She is gifted with a good voice and a photogenic appearance. "I look better on TV than I do in real life." she says. "I always think people are disappointed when they meet me."

After nine months at the station in Houston, where she learned the technical aspects of her job, Linda was offered a job at the network's flagship station in New York. For many TV reporters, New York is the Big Apple, and not only because of better pay. Her work in New York attracted another network, which offered her a network job in Washington, D.C.

Each network produces a news program that its affiliates use in the evening and, in some cases, the morning. The network news is directed at a broader audience and tends to cover events of national interest. Local stations concentrate on happenings in the immediate area. Network jobs are highly coveted and highly paid.

In New York Linda was expected to do one story a day. Betsy, at a smaller station in Washington, D.C., must do two. At even smaller stations, the reporter might be expected not only to report the news, but to write it, edit the film, script the program, and anchor the show.

Stories are assigned by editors or suggested by reporters. As on newspapers, the good reporter has initiative and imagination and always has a list of at least ten stories she would like to do if she only had time.

One evening Linda's producer received a phone call from a night watchman at a cottage once lived in by Edgar Allan Poe. The night watchman said that the cottage was in disrepair and neglected, although it was a National Park Service landmark. He suggested their doing a story.

Linda was sent out that night with a camera crew. She interviewed the watchman and filmed the house at night. The next day she returned with the camera crew to film the cracks in the walls, broken steps, and tumbledown furniture by daylight. She also interviewed a custodian and some local children, who admitted having vandalized the cottage.

Back at the station, Linda called Park Service officials to ask why the cottage had been neglected. Earlier calls had elicited the promise of a spokesman to meet her at the cottage in the morning—but only the custodian had appeared.

Then she viewed the morning's film and the previous evening's footage with the associate producer. They discussed which film to use and what the story would say. The story would be two minutes and forty-five seconds long, with a twenty-second "live tag" that Linda would read from the news program set during the show.

While the associate producer supervised the film cutting and reassembling, Linda wrote the script of her story. In the interim, she had gone off to tape a regular feature on "100 years ago today" that each reporter was assigned to do in turn for the station.

By 4:45 the script was written and the story nearly complete. It included film of the cottage and the interviews, a "voice over" narration, and the "live" ending. The story would be the sixteenth item on the news program.

After the broadcast, Linda went home to New Jersey, where her two children had prepared a surprise birthday party for her. She has a live-in housekeeper, for with the unpredictability of her hours, she cannot rely on baby-sitters.

On the late news Linda's story was cut slightly. It was considered timely and interesting enough, however, to remain on the news, while other stories were cut entirely.

"I have no doubt that I got my job because I'm a woman," she said. "They had a quota they had to fill. But I love this work: it's a great job. I don't know what lies in my future—it remains to be seen whether they will allow women to grow old on television the way men do."

Betsy Ashton's day at the smaller television station involves fewer people and more stories. As a rule, she goes out on one assignment in the morning and returns to the station to complete the story. Then she has another assignment in the afternoon. Her station's news broadcast is at 10 P.M., so there is a little more time before the deadline.

Print reporters and television reporters tend to be rivals. Newspaper people often resent the television crews and their awkward equipment, particularly when a press conference is delayed while a television crew sets up lights and cameras. Print reporters may complain that television reporters value pizzazz more than truth; that they don't prepare for press conferences and, consequently, ask dumb, time-consuming questions. In their rush to film someone or something, film crews often push pen-and-pad reporters out of the way with their cameras.

Some television people, on the other hand, feel that their print colleagues lack understanding of a TV reporter's difficulty in managing all the elements—the film, the sound, the story—of a TV piece. They envy the comparative length a newspaper person has for a story and a print reporter's ability to go into greater depth. But they also complain that newspaper stories are boring and that most people don't read them.

"Print people complain that we ask dumb questions," Linda Ellerbee said. "Well, I'll ask a dumb question four times if I have to—it's the answer I need on film, not the question. A newspaper reporter can quote "sources," but if I don't have someone on camera or tape, it's useless to me. And I think more people are willing to talk to a newspaper reporter than to appear on television."

Broadcasting is an exciting and glamorous business. It is also a pressured business, and the mortality rate is high.

If you want to get into broadcasting, the best way to prepare is with a good general education and as many journalism courses as you can include. And get experience. Talking on television or radio is totally unlike conversation, even though television and radio personalities appear to do it easily.

When you are choosing a college, consider the broadcasting facilities carefully. More and more schools are adding television and radio stations to their campus resources. Experience on these stations can be invaluable. Look at the outlets in your own town. Do they have any internship programs? Do they need anyone to help out around the station without pay?

Experience with a print medium can't hurt but is not really necessary to the successful radio or television journalist, because the styles are so different.

Learn as much as you can about all aspects of broadcasting. Even if your heart's dream is to be the female Walter Cronkite, it is important to know every part of the process of broadcast news—how it happens and why. Learn about film and start listening to your own voice. Tape yourself reading news stories and listen carefully to how you sound. If your diction is sloppy, your voice screechy, or your accent an impediment to comprehension, you may need to invest in speech lessons.

Take every opportunity you can to appear on television or radio. Sometimes local stations invite high school students to appear on the public affairs programs that are shown on Sunday morning. Whatever it is, do it.

6

Trade Journals and
Other Publications

Although the word "journalism" usually suggests newspaper work or news broadcasting, there are many
trained journalists working for other types of publications. These publications range from special interest
magazines and newspapers to newsletters to alternative
newspapers. All offer opportunities for employment that
any aspiring journalist should consider.

Some of these are called "house organs." Almost
every large organization, whether in government or in
private industry, publishes one. They are small newspapers for the employees of the organization. They contain feature stories about employee achievements, news
about the company, classified ads, and notices of up-
coming events. They are usually produced by small staffs
who report, write, edit, and design the publication
themselves.

Specialty magazines are another source of work. There
are more than 500 periodicals relating to agriculture
alone. There are 80 Jewish publications, 558 other reli-

gious magazines, and more than 6,300 other magazines on subjects ranging from folk dancing to aviation.

Virtually every profession, from undertakers to the police, has its "trade journal." Some fields have several. These publications may offer nothing but pleasant stories about their own readers—promoting their own businesses —but many are serious magazines. They keep subscribers informed of new developments in their field and of legislation relating to it.

For a list of 2,380 business publications compiled by the American Business Press write to them at 205 East 42 Street, New York, N.Y. 10017. They also publish a free booklet, *Careers in the Business Press,* which might be helpful.

Another source of publications is the *Ayer Directory of Publications,* which can be found in most public libraries. This hefty book lists 23,000 publications in the United States and Canada—probably every publication that exists. They are listed by name, by type, and by state.

Trade or special interest magazines can offer the advantage of regular hours. Newspapers and television make a heavy demand on one's private life, with the constant unpredictability of news. Aside from the occasional emergency that happens anywhere, an employee of such magazines can usually say "I'll be home for dinner at seven," and mean it.

Another advantage is the chance to specialize, to become an expert in a particular field. This expertise can, with individual initiative, lead to free-lance articles for mass audience publications.

Judi Bredemeier has found happiness with a trade publication. A graduate of Indiana University's journalism school, she had worked summers on two newspapers as a general assignment reporter. She had also worked on the daily campus paper.

Judi is now the managing editor of *Travel Management Daily* and *Travel Management Newsletter,* two of seven travel publications put out by the Reuben H. Donnelly Corp. Before her promotion to managing editor, she was a reporter in Donnelly's Washington bureau, covering the Civil Aeronautics Board, the Department of Transportation, and other government agencies whose actions had an effect on the travel industry.

As a reporter, she filed at least one story every day for a 5 P.M. deadline. She also wrote feature stories for the other publications—*TravelScene* (circulation about 100,000), *TravelAge East (*circulation 13,000), *Travel-Age West* (circulation 12,000), and *TravelAge Mid-America* (circulation 9,000). The magazines' subscribers are travel agents, transportation industry executives, hotel industry executives, and other business people involved in travel.

The *Daily* is read by high-level industry executives. It provides hard-news reports on travel industry concerns —government actions, airline innovations, and so forth. It is two pages long; stories must be short and concise. The four-page *Newsletter* is published twice a week and is directed at mid-level management. There is no advertising in either publication.

As managing editor, Judi directs a staff of six in New York. She employs reporters in Chicago, Los Angeles, San Francisco, Honolulu, Washington, and London. She supervises the paste up, edits copy, makes assignments, and in general runs the whole operation.

"I never realized how important a publication like this can be," she said. "People are actually making high-level company decisions on the basis of information they read in the *Daily*. I consider my competition to be *The New York Times* and the *Wall Street Journal*. It upsets me if they have a travel story we don't, and it delights me to beat them. Usually we're a step ahead."

One major advantage of the job for her is the opportunity to travel. Since going to work for the company, she has visited almost every country in Europe and Asia. Once she spent a month in Indonesia, covering the Pacific Area Travel Congress. In one year she went to Ireland three times: the first time she covered a conference on the energy crisis for the *Daily,* the second time she wrote a feature story on what to do and where to go in Ireland for the *TravelAge* magazines, and the third time she wrote a profile of Aer Lingus (the Irish airline) for *TravelScene*.

I love the traveling—there isn't much point in working for a travel magazine if you don't. But I've noticed that we still haven't gotten to the point where people don't raise their eyebrows at your leaving your husband to fend for himself for two weeks.

People on planes will say to me, "You mean your husband *lets* you travel by yourself?" and I say, "You mean your wife *lets* you?" They seem to think it's okay for a husband to travel on business, but not for a wife.

The managing editor job was a promotion. It meant that Judi had to move to New York. Her husband works in Washington. They commute on the weekends. Despite the raised eyebrows of their families and some of their friends, they find it a reasonable arrangement for the time being.

"I always wanted to be a newspaper reporter," Judi

said. "I never would have imagined I'd work for an industry publication. But the work is very like newspaper work. It's really a dream job. The travel industry has a vacation atmosphere, but the work is challenging."

Apparently quite a few people think it might be a dream job. An unsigned advertisement seeking a replacement for Judi when she became managing editor drew 700 applications. She herself had been chosen from among 500 applicants three and a half years earlier.

The reporter who got the job is a 30-year-old woman with years of experience working for UPI, including covering the war in Vietnam.

There are other special interest publications that exist to express a particular point of view or provide an alternative to establishment media.

Majority Report, for example, is a bimonthly newspaper for women published in New York by a small and low-paid staff. In Washington the *D.C. Gazette* and a new paper, *Newsworks,* cover city politics and the arts. The stories are clearly shaped by personal opinions, and sometimes contain valuable city news that Washington's two large newspapers either can't or won't cover.

Alternative media used to be known as "underground" newspapers. They appeared irregularly and were known for radical philosophies or outrageous story ideas and a concentration on the arts. Today, alternative papers are generally staffed by experienced professionals, and they offer investigative reporting, consumer news, and a different approach to the news as well as arts reviews and interviews. There are about fifty such publications, but their number varies almost monthly because of the generally precarious situations of their low budgets.

Linda Matys is the managing editor of the *Valley Advocate*, a successful weekly paper published in western Massachusetts and Connecticut. The paper was started with less than $5,000 by Linda's husband and a friend a few years ago. All three had experience in daily or weekly "regular" journalism and wanted to publish a paper that would appeal to the many college-age people in the Amherst area.

Now the paper is published in three cities, Amherst, Massachusetts, and Hartford and New Haven, Connecticut. It began with an unpaid staff of overworked volunteers, including Linda and the two publishers. The paper now employs about fifty people and pays everyone $120 a week. The paper is distributed free. All revenue comes from advertisements. (Even newspapers that are sold get most of their income from advertisements.)

"We've started calling ourselves a weekly paper rather than an alternative paper, although that's still on the masthead," Linda said.

What we're doing is not that much different from what large papers like the Boston *Globe* are doing. There aren't any papers in this area covering issues in as much depth as we do. We are consumer-oriented and like to get into controversial issues. The writing is much more important here than on a daily. I don't edit out subjective or reactive stuff for example. We may take a stance on an issue and expect the reporter to write almost a narrative. We did a story about the state mental hospital near here and the reporter wrote a sidebar about his experience on going through the hospital the first time.

We put great emphasis on writing style. It's really creative and demanding. We have to make sense and have some impact; we don't just churn it out.

Linda said that while the staff is "doing it for love," the paper is not a "hippie commune" but a serious business. Decisions are not made collectively, although reporters influence what the paper covers or emphasizes.

"One thing that makes alternative journalism attractive is that people are more willing to teach you because they can't pay you much. They may spend half an hour going over a story and helping you to improve. It's a good way for an inexperienced person to get started. We're always interested in a responsible volunteer.

"We like to say that you trade money for freedom," she said. Linda has a master's degree in English and a year's experience as the woman's editor of a small weekly paper, a job she got by responding to an ad in another newspaper. She has also taught journalism in high school and moderated a public television show on women. The first year of the paper's existence she had to supplement her income by working in a federally funded program for the deaf. Now she works seven days a week editing the paper, which has expanded its audience well beyond the college crowd. For Linda, "overwork is a way of life." But she seems to like it that way.

Linda plans to have children. She expects to curtail her work at the paper when she does, perhaps doing occasional writing and "picking up the odds and ends that haven't been done." The relaxed style of an alternative paper might lend itself to a freer schedule or the possibility of bringing one's infant to the office instead of hiring a baby-sitter. However, Linda said that the work is too emotionally demanding to sustain and yet have enough creative energy left over to give to a child.

"You're so exposed on a small paper like this," she said. "There is a strong tie with the readers. People come up to you on the street and say they love the paper or they hate it. It takes commitment, which is hard to wean yourself from."

Most of the five reporters who work for the *Valley Advocate* have several years' experience on daily newspapers, although the publishers hired one straight out of college. Free-lancing is one way of getting published in such papers. They're usually looking for good material at small prices.

"Basically, it's a tremendously exciting and satisfying way of life," Linda added.

Syndicates

Work for a syndicate is another kind of journalism. Syndicates are organizations that contract with newspapers to provide columnists or features on a regular basis. In this way a newspaper can get specialized writing at less expense than by hiring their own staff person. The syndicate earns money by selling the same product to many newspapers in different locations.

Many syndicates use only columnists, such as Ann Landers, Erma Bombeck, and Sylvia Porter. It would be impossible for anyone without writing experience to be a syndicated columnist—that is a position earned after years of local or national exposure in a particular field.

Other syndicates send out stories written either by their own staff members or "stringers," who are generally people with reporting or writing experience.

Features and News Service is an example of a syndicate, although an unusual one. It was started in 1968 by an experienced Chicago newswoman, Colleen Dishon, and her husband, Bob. Its intention was to serve the "woman's section in transition." At that time some newspapers were starting to change their so-called women's section from a fashion and society feature to a department of more general interest. Papers wanted stories about the women's movement, consumer issues, lifestyles, and news about education and other issues. They were not equipped to write them "in-house." This was —and is—a void that Features and News expects to fill.

The service now has forty client newspapers all over the country. Each week it mails a package of four or five stories written by the service's four staff writers (two in Washington, D.C., and two in Chicago) or one of its stringers. Clients pay a monthly retainer and can use the stories as they wish, as well as the pictures that are sent with the stories.

Pat Anstett is one of the two staff members based in Washington. She moved to Washington in January 1974 when her husband got a better job than the one he'd had in Chicago. Pat is a graduate of Michigan State's journalism school, where she also worked on the daily campus paper. After college she worked for six years on daily newspapers in Chicago, covering hard news as well as features.

After moving to Washington, she worked for six months at *Congressional Quarterly,* which she found stuffy and conservative. She began working as a stringer for Features and News and became a full-time reporter in June 1975.

Now she works out of an office in the basement of her home. She keeps her own "morgue" of newspaper and magazine clippings and is assisted only by a $100 telephone answering machine. Pat writes several stories a week, concentrating on child development, consumer news, women's issues, and features.

> I make my own schedule. I can put in a load of wash between phone calls if I want. It does take a lot of discipline and sometimes I miss the office atmosphere. But then I don't have the office distractions, either. The disadvantage is that there is no immediate feedback from people: I'm never sure how good a story is, because if a paper doesn't use the story you never know why. I would not recommend this kind of work for an inexperienced person—you need to work in a structured situation and have help the first few years, no matter how good you are.

One great satisfaction for Pat is not having to answer to a daily deadline. "When I was working for a newspaper I never had time to do more than interview someone and check the clips. Now I can go to the library and check journals and read books and do pieces that are far more comprehensive."

Pat wants children and hopes that her home-office lifestyle will prove to be as flexible as she thinks it might be. "I'm hoping that I will be able to hire a baby-sitter a couple of days a week and schedule all my interviews on those days," she said, "although a lot of women I've talked to say they end up hiring one full-time because there are so many interruptions at home."

In addition to her work for Features and News, Pat has written free-lance articles for the *Washingtonian* and the *National Observer*. "I think this would be very hard to do without experience," she said. "I have, now, seven years. Unless you have a name it's very difficult to get free-lance assignments. You really have to have a reputation and you can only develop that by beginning locally."

Whatever the form—trade journal, special interest magazine, alternative media, or syndicate—the skills required are the same. Accurate reporting, a clear, concise writing style, and the ability to perform editing chores are as much in demand at these organizations as they are at a major newspaper or newsmagazine.

7

Free-Lance Writing

Most magazine articles are written by free-lance writers who are commissioned by the publication's editor. Some magazines employ researchers and hire a few staff writers who are paid a regular salary. Others retain writers as "contributing editors," perhaps paying them a regular fee or giving them a contract for a specific number of stories.

Many newspapers employ "stringers," correspondents who report from special areas or cover special subjects on a part-time basis. Newspaper stringers are often paid "space rates"—on the basis of word-count. Newspapers rarely pay as well as magazines for free-lance work.

Free-lancing is one of the most precarious ways to make a living. Without an official link to any one organization, a free-lancer's income can fluctuate greatly from one year to the next. A few free-lancers make a lot of money; many make enough to live on. Most don't make enough to cover their expenses.

Nonetheless, free-lancing is appealing to many people. It offers freedom, independence, and—especially attractive to mothers of young children—a chance to work at home. Once you have established a reputation you can choose your assignments, accepting only those that interest you.

The way to successful free-lancing is paved with rejection slips. One editor dislikes your idea; another has already assigned someone to the same story; a third doesn't even answer your letter.

It is not wise to begin a free-lancing career without any other source of income. Many editors and reporters write articles in addition to their regular jobs; some find markets for pieces regularly enough so that they can—if they want to—quit their jobs and concentrate on independent work.

Phyllis Richman is a free lance in Washington, D.C., who has been able, over a three-year period, to build up a clientele who give her regular assignments. She could not have done it without her husband's support during the first two lean years. Now that she is expecting to make nearly $20,000 a year, her husband is thinking about taking it easier, and possibly doing some writing as well.

Phyllis writes about food and restaurants. She does a regular column called "Try It" for the Washington *Post*'s Sunday magazine. She is a contributing editor for *Washingtonian* magazine and has written for *Esquire*.

"The first thing I learned was that it is important to get into print somewhere, anywhere," she said. "The first thing I wrote was a restaurant column for a Jewish newspaper. They didn't pay me anything. But it gave me confidence and the credentials to start approaching other publications. Then things started to snowball. Now I have more work than I can handle."

Phyllis has three children. She likes to be there when

they get home from school but sometimes interviews make that impossible. She and her husband rent the top floor of their house to a student couple who are available for baby-sitting. On Monday she tries to schedule appointments and baby-sitting for the week.

She works about fifty hours a week on her free-lance articles and usually has three or four in preparation. She has learned to use her time when she has it, make telephone calls during the day and sometimes write in the evening.

"I have a tendency to over-research and let things pile up," she said. "I end up doing a lot of writing on weekends. It's like constant exam time."

She finds that working at home creates problems other than the lack of office camaraderie that some free-lance writers miss. "It's very hard to establish the officialness of your office when you work at home," she said. "Friends and relatives feel free to call you up anytime to chat, which they probably wouldn't do if I worked downtown."

Although she says she's not as well-organized as she'd like to be, Phyllis has learned some things about free-lancing that are good advice:

Never send an editor a story; send a query first. You might begin a letter of query with the proposed lead for a story. Then you present the idea and your qualifications for doing it. Don't give them too many facts because stealing ideas has been known to happen. Don't mention money in the query.

Keep a lot of story ideas going at once; that way one rejection doesn't bother you so much. I've learned to be philosophical about rejections—you never know why someone has rejected your idea, really. It could be because one editor is having a war with another.

Keep lists of everyone you telephone while you're

doing a story. Sometimes I make fifty phone calls and when they start calling back I forget what I called them about.

Get every story commitment in writing from the editor, with the fee named. Keep track of all your expenses while doing a story. On some stories your expenses will be paid. Otherwise you can use them as a tax deduction.

Always get your story in on time, on the exact day you promised it. This seems to be very important. More than once I've found that an article of mine was used because another free-lance writer missed a deadline.

I sometimes have to push people to pay me what they owe me. At first this made me uncomfortable—I still don't like having to do it—but some magazines are always behind. You just have to keep at them.

Keep a file on every story and a running list of what you're doing for whom and how much they owe you.

When you're talking to an editor for the first time, be confident but not cocky.

One reason that Phyllis has been successful is that she has specialized in one field. She has a reputation for excellence in that area. She's reliable and quick, and local editors like to use her.

Sometimes a query to an editor will get you an assignment, with an expense advance offered and a "kill fee" stipulated. A kill fee is a sum that the magazine will pay you if the article is not used.

Never submit an idea or an article to more than one magazine at once. But, once it is rejected, submit it to someone else immediately—what's wrong for one editor may be just right for another.

Magazine articles are usually longer than newspaper articles and are expected to deal with a subject in more depth. Sentences and paragraphs can be longer than for a newspaper, and personal style is permitted—sometimes demanded.

A magazine writer must be a self-starter. This means having the ability to work by yourself, to produce without an editor looking over your shoulder or the pressure of a daily deadline. A lot of people find this very difficult; consider carefully the strength of your self-discipline before you decide to try free-lancing.

Several publications list magazines that publish free-lance articles, extremely helpful to know for a person trying to make a go of free-lance writing.

Writer's Market is one. In 1,000 pages it lists some 5,000 outlets for free-lancers and a description of the kind of articles the editors want. We've already mentioned the *Ayer Directory,* which is even more comprehensive. *Literary Market Place* lists names and addresses of various magazines by name and subject matter, as well as associations for writers. Although primarily directed at the book publishing market, *LMP* is a useful reference generally available in your local library.

The Writer's Yearbook is published annually and prints articles of interest to free-lance writers. A recent issue, for example, had stories ranging from "How to Research for the Specialized Markets" to "Collecting Checks from the Hobby Magazines."

Financially, Phyllis Richman has been extraordinarily successful. Free-lancers should expect to make no more than a few hundred dollars when they start out. Some publications pay nothing—just a chance to get into print. Others may pay $15 or $20, while the *Reader's Digest* pays $2,000 or $3,000 an article, generally considered the plum of the free-lance writer's market in terms of money.

8

Public Relations, Public Information, and Government Jobs

The field of public relations has its own public relations problem. The phrase has become almost a synonym for the whitewash of an organization's problems or for shameless self-promotion. The field certainly includes practitioners of such dubious arts, but it also involves a range of legitimate duties and skills.

Although the field is relatively new, more and more companies, organizations, and governments are finding it necessary to employ a public relations person. In some cases these people are really in the field of public information. It is important to know the differences between the two types of jobs. Generally, public relations jobs are closely related to advertising skills, while public information is a field closely allied to journalism.

Public Relations

If you consult the list of journalism schools at the end of this book, you'll see that 101 schools and universities offer courses in public relations or practical experience in the field.

In its simplest form, the public relations person is the link between an organization and the public. The job may involve answering letters, public speaking, writing newsletters, getting information for reporters, holding press conferences, advising company policymakers on the public impact of various decisions or advertising campaigns, or writing press releases.

Most of these tasks involve journalistic skills. They also demand a person who likes people, one who is outgoing and personable as well as skilled. The public relations person is often in the position of representing the organization she works for—of being its public image. This may be why women have not often been given the top public relations jobs until recently—men were thought to present a more responsible image.

A good P.R. person does research on whatever task she has—in other words, reporting—and presents only information that is accurate and up-to-date. Although the public relations person will probably never be presenting negative information about her employers, if reporters ask specific questions a good P.R. person learns either to give out the facts or to say honestly "I can't get you that."

Public relations can be fun because it involves so many skills. In one day you might be selecting photographs, writing a press release, and editing a company publication.

There are public relations firms as well as departments in individual companies. You may have noticed that most theater programs include the credit "press relations." A P.R. firm may be hired for a specific job, to promote a Broadway show, for example. It is responsible for pre-opening publicity, setting up interviews with the director or the stars, answering questions from the media about the show, and, perhaps, arranging the opening-night party. Some firms are also involved in the advertising and the design of posters for the show.

According to U.S. Census figures, 20,182 women were in public relations or publicity writing in 1970 (compared with 55,416 men). Ten years before, the number of women was a paltry 7,271 (compared with 23,870 men). Although the gap between the numbers of men and women employed has widened, the increased percentage of women in the field perhaps indicates that doors are opening.

Public relations usually pays more than newspaper work. The hours are fairly regular. There are opportunities to meet a lot of people and use writing, editing, and broadcast skills. You can also have an effect on policy. In many organizations the public relations executive is part of the top-level decision-making team.

If the world of business doesn't appeal to you, there are also jobs in noncommercial public relations—with church groups, political organizations, avant-guard theater groups, or nonprofit organizations involved in such areas as population control or world peace. In these days of media consciousness, even radical political groups have "spokespersons" or someone with the responsibility of communicating the group's message most effectively to the public.

Public Information

For a person trained as a reporter, a job in public information (P.I.) may be more satisfying than one in public relations. Most of these jobs are with a local, state, or federal government agency.

While the job may involve writing press releases and newsletters as in public relations, a public information person is also often asked to provide answers to specific questions from either the media or the public. These questions can range from interpretation of official policy to the birth date of an organization official.

Press releases must be written as concisely as news stories and deal with everything from new appointments and summaries of the annual budget to information on where to register to vote. Public information people also send the media notices of an organization's accomplishments or services.

Cheryl Everett is a Citizen Communication Assistant for the city of Pontiac, Michigan. There are three more people in the communications office—a supervisor, a photographer, and a secretary. They are responsible for dispensing information about the city and its services, promoting the image of Pontiac, and running a municipal complaint bureau.

Cheryl produces a newsletter called the *Quarter-Pulse,* which comes out four times a year. It is mailed to 26,000 residents with their water bills. She writes the copy, plans the layout, decides what pictures the photographer should take, delivers the four-page product to the printer, checks the proof sheets, and oversees the printing.

The newsletter contains items of interest to Pontiac citizens, ranging from notices of bicentennial events to progress reports of downtown development. "Crime statistics have been a big story too," Cheryl says. "We've actually had a decrease in crime—and Pontiac is one of the few cities to experience this."

Cheryl must also write press releases to send to news organizations in the area. (Pontiac is about thirty miles from Detroit.) Releases are sent to about fifteen radio and television stations, twelve newspapers, and ten municipal publications in other cities. She helped write the application that won Pontiac the All-America City of 1975 award.

But Cheryl said her proudest accomplishment is the recent establishment of "Dial-A-News." This is a ninety-second recording of city news and information that is available by telephone. It was Cheryl's idea. She says that it was the first of its kind in the country.

The project was exciting for her because she did everything from purchasing the recording equipment to writing and taping the broadcasts. She is also the announcer who reads the information. The first tape included reports on the fifth anniversary of the city's methadone clinic, clean-up progress after a major ice storm, the agenda of the next day's city commission meeting, and an update on a sewer construction project. She was proud to report that six hundred citizens called "Dial-A-News" the first day, with only a small amount of publicity preceding the inauguration of what is now a daily fixture.

Cheryl majored in history in college, although she was interested in journalism. "I edited the newspaper and the yearbook in high school, but when I got to college I found they didn't offer any journalism courses," she said. "But I don't think I missed anything. My training was more or less learn as you work."

While in college, she worked as an aide to a Michigan state legislator, a job that led to her first "real" job after school, working for a nonprofit housing corporation in

Detroit. The job included public relations work and writing a newsletter. Through it she met the Pontiac official who offered her her present job in 1972.

> I always thought I wanted to be a reporter. I somehow thought reporters were more servants of the people. But since I've been in public information that distinction has become blurry. I feel strongly that we play an important role in the life of the city. People are always complaining about how citizens don't get involved, or that they don't know what's going on. Well, we're letting people know what's going on in their government. We translate things so that people can understand what's happening, instead of trying to deal with an unintelligible bureaucracy.

Cheryl and her husband, who is studying for a graduate degree in music, live in a house they recently purchased in nearby Waterford. At a salary of $16,500 a year, she is making more money than most newspaper reporters, another factor in choosing public information over journalism.

After her husband gets his degree, Cheryl hopes to start her own business as a consultant in municipal public relations and information. Now thirty, she plans to have children once her business is started. She thinks the flexibility of being her own boss will give her a chance to work and raise her family at the same time.

As one of only three women who have top-level jobs in the city government, she is concerned about opportunities for other women. "The city was forced to design an affirmative action plan, but unfortunately it provides only for hiring more women and minorities and doesn't say anything about promotions," she said. "Aside from that, I don't feel I've had any problems as a woman in my career."

Press Secretaries

The press secretary of a public official has one of the most glamorous journalism-related jobs. The work ranges from writing and editing to making arrangements for a press conference.

Many press secretaries are former reporters, attracted either by a particular candidate, a high salary, or the excitement of the job. Some reporters, fed up with the "objective" work of news-gathering, find greater satisfaction in communicating the views of someone who stands for something, who creates news, or who is a leader.

Jean McDonald is the press secretary for Rep. Joseph L. Fisher (Democrat, Virginia), who unseated a congressman people thought unbeatable in 1974.

After graduating in journalism from Stanford University, Jean worked for three and a half years for the California State Bar Association as a public relations specialist. Then she married a reporter and about a year and a half later had her first child. For the next eighteen years, she decided to be a full-time mother and housewife, limiting her "professional" life to writing the community newsletter or press releases for her children's nursery school.

As a press secretary on Capitol Hill, Jean is responsible for writing and editing a newsletter for constituents, answering some mail, helping to write speeches, writing press releases, answering questions from reporters, and, most importantly, keeping track of her boss's activities and positions on different issues.

This job is not like working for the president of a bank. It's a very personal relationship and has to do with who he is, what he is, and his whole approach. In a sense I'm like a reporter always interviewing him. I'm always taking notes on what he says. In some offices the press secretary is creating the congressman, but that isn't the case here.

On days before the newsletter deadline, I may work from 7:30 A.M. to 7:30 P.M. Other days it's 9:30 A.M. to 6:30 P.M. Some days I am totally immersed in researching one subject, like the Concorde SST. Then, sure enough, the first call is about strip mining or the Equal Rights Amendment.

The hardest thing for me was learning to set priorities. I try to call every reporter back as soon as I can, but when it comes to divvying up the congressman's time, a call from a local paper is more important than one from Ohio.

In dealing with reporters, Jean is very conscious of a press secretary's responsibility to be accurate, reliable, and responsive. "The most important thing is judgment," she said. "I'm not going to call up reporters about every little thing; I decide what events or issues are worth a reporter's attention. Otherwise they start to ignore you. And, of course, the local weeklies are more interested in local issues than the national dailies. And I always try to be fair—leaking something to one reporter may earn you anger from the others."

Although she is now committed to having a full-time job, she does not regret the years she spent homemaking. "I don't see how women with young children do it," she said. "When I come home I'm exhausted. I don't feel like cooking dinner or mopping the floor. And I feel very strongly that someone should be at home when the children are little."

Her husband had been a reporter for United Press (now United Press International) when their children were young. He worked from 3 P.M. to midnight. "If you were lucky they'd let you know a week in advance what your days off would be," she said. "If I'd had a full-time job we might never have seen each other."

Jean started her new career at the bottom—as a volunteer stuffing envelopes for Fisher's first local campaign. Later she did volunteer press work for him and another candidate. When Fisher decided to run for Congress, Jean became Communications Director at $80 a month.

At this point, she changed her life-style. She asked her two daughters (both teen-agers at this point) to help out more with the housework. Her husband now does the grocery shopping and shares other household chores.

Looking back on her education, Jean said that her most valuable experience was student work on the Stanford daily newspaper. She still uses what she learned there—layout, editing, and writing. The experience of a daily deadline gave her invaluable understanding of reporters' and editors' problems.

Lately she has discovered that the difference between broadcast and print media affects the reporting of her boss's views. He is a congressman interested in complex technical issues, which are not easily explained in the simple format of broadcast journalism. Fisher's views are sometimes misrepresented or distorted by reporters, she said. Jean is trying to improve her releases to broadcast reporters by clarifying and simplifying the writing in order to forestall these problems.

Fisher, like most congressmen, writes articles and columns for newspapers in his district, which Jean usually reviews. She has some voice in policy decisions. Because she basically respects and shares her boss's philosophy, they've had few disagreements over issues.

"If we had a serious disagreement I'd have to think

about leaving," she said. "I don't think this is the kind of job where you should stay on if you truly object to what you have to report to others."

Government Jobs

Aside from municipal government jobs, such as Cheryl Everett's, there are almost 4,300 federal government jobs in the field of journalism. About 2,400 of these are in public information offices, while another 1,900 are writing and/or editing jobs.

Although about 75 percent of these federal jobs are in Washington, D.C., the rest are located all over the country and the world.

"We are informing the public about programs and policies, not just building the public image," said John Moore, who works in the public information office of the Civil Service Commission.

Moore said that federal jobs are in great demand, and only experienced people are hired for the best ones. With an average salary of $16,255—and a top level salary of $37,800—the government can attract experienced journalists. Nevertheless, between fifty and sixty jobs become available each year—and the government is an equal opportunity employer!

Moore gives countless talks to classes of young people interested in federal careers in journalism. He recommends at least a B.A. in journalism for anyone seeking such a career. Further, he advises young people to get government job experience through a work-study program or summer internships (more about these in Chapter 10, Job-Hunting).

The United States Information Agency, for example, publishes sixteen magazines, seven of them produced in this country and nine overseas. The magazines produced here include *Economic Quarterly, America Illustrated,* and *Problems of Communism.* Free-lance pieces by well-known authorities are used, but the magazines are produced for the most part by staff writers, editors, and reporters. The magazines are all directed at foreign readers. The agency's job is to communicate this country's culture and policies to people overseas.

There is a summer internship program in the press and publications section of the agency for college students or recent graduates. Two or three young people are selected through applications. They spend the summer reporting, writing, or editing. Application for full-time jobs begins with the written Civil Service exam. If you pass it, you take an oral exam. There have been as many as 6,000 applicants for twelve jobs.

The Voice of America is the radio network of USIA. It broadcasts twenty-four hours a day to different countries around the world in thirty-five languages. A central newsroom in the Washington headquarters produces news programs based on reports from its own correspondents and from news services. They are written and announced by staff broadcasters. Other departments produce radio shows of feature stories, interviews, and music. The VOA has twenty-three studios in Washington, three in New York, and one each in Miami, Los Angeles, and Chicago.

Other government agencies employ writers and editors to produce pamphlets, brochures, and reports as well as to work in public information offices. It is not necessary for a person to agree with every official government action to work for the government. Such uniformity of viewpoint would be impossible to assemble from so many employees even if it was desired. As with any job, however, there is no point in accepting employment with the government if your political feelings would create continual crises of conscience for you on the job.

The first step toward any career job in government is to take the P.A.C.E.—Professional Administrative Career Examination. There is no fee for taking this test. School placement offices or your local state employment office can tell you when and where it is given in your area.

Your score on this test (which is something like the Graduate Record Exam or the College Boards) is placed on a federal register. When a vacancy is available, your application and test score are evaluated, and you may be called for an interview.

A beginning-level employee would probably earn about $8,900 a year.

Surprisingly, 39 percent of federal journalism jobs are in the Department of Defense, according to Moore. The Department of Health, Education and Welfare has the second largest contingent of public information specialists. Some offices consist of one career officer and a secretary, while others are vast information-producing operations. Women have served in top positions in such diverse departments as the Johnson Space Center in Houston, the Department of Housing and Urban Development, and the White House.

9

Women in American
Journalism

Although women journalists have only come into their
own during the past two decades, many courageous
women ventured earlier into the field despite social
disapproval and discrimination.

You will not read about many of these women in
journalism texts even though women have been involved in journalism since before the American Revo-
lution.

Benjamin Franklin's publishing activities are well-
known. But did you know that his sister-in-law, Ann
Franklin, helped to publish Rhode Island's first successful newspaper, the *Newport Mercury*? She was also
made that colony's official printer.

Mary Katherine Goddard helped her brother found
Maryland's second newspaper, the *Maryland Journal*.
She published it alone during the Revolutionary War
and until 1784. Her mother, Sarah Updike Goddard,
published the *Providence Gazette*.

In the mid-1830s two attempts at publishing a
"woman's paper" were made briefly in New York. One

was called *Woman,* published by one Ann Oddbody. The other was the *Ladies Morning Star,* published by William Newell, who also published the *Sun,* the *Herald,* and the *Tribune* in the same city. The *Star* was supposed to be a "literary, Moral Newspaper . . . that may improve and adorn the female mind." Both papers folded because advertisers shunned them.

The first woman to "integrate" the all-male Capitol press gallery in Washington was Jane Swisshelm, who invaded it for a day in 1850 while visiting Washington as a columnist for the *Pittsburgh Saturday Visiter.* She wrote later:

> No woman had ever had a place in the Congressional reporters'. This door I wanted to open to them, so I called on vice-president Fillmore and asked him to assign me a seat in the Senate gallery. He was much surprised and tried to dissuade me. The place would be very unpleasant for a lady, would attract attention, I would not like it; but he gave me the seat. . . .

In 1877 women were banned from the Capitol press gallery for fourteen years. Then Isabel Worrell Ball received credentials, and women have been accepted there ever since.

The first woman reporter hired by *The New York Times* was, as far as we know, Midy Morgan, a tall Irishwoman who walked with a limp and carried a gun. Known as a character, she covered the livestock beat after being hired in 1869. The same year Sally Joy was hired by the Boston *Post* as a society reporter.

The beginnings of what became the "women's page" started during the 1850s with two columnists, Fanny Fern and Jenny June (in those days women journalists often used pseudonyms). They wrote about recipes, fashion, and "morals," and both writers became very popular.

In the late 1800s women were often employed for "stunt journalism," a gimmick familiar even today. One of the most famous stunt journalists was Nellie Bly, whose real name was Elizabeth Cochrane.

Nellie persuaded the New York *World* to send her on a trip around the world in an attempt to break the record proposed in Jules Verne's novel *Around the World in 80 Days*. When she returned after 72 days, 6 hours, and 11 minutes, having covered 24,899 miles, she became a popular heroine. Later she pretended insanity in order to write about an asylum—a technique used by Washington *Post* reporter Karlyn Barker as recently as 1972.

Sometime during the first part of the twentieth century women journalists became known as "sob sisters." As described by Adela Rogers St. John, one of the best-known of them, ". . . the idea of a sob sister, unlike that of the objective reporter, was to walk right into the experience. To reach hearts, you have to do more than report the facts."

Their stories were emotional and sensational. Many were inspired by some cause, such as saving a building or raising money for a pathetic destitute. The writers made no pretense of objectivity but took a point of view and carried their readers along with them. As recently as 1976 Mrs. St. John was still at work, called out of retirement to cover the trial of Patty Hearst, whose grandfather William Randolph Hearst had been her boss for much of her life.

The suffrage movement also gave women opportunities to cover hard news instead of the feature writing most had been limited to. Years later, the feminist movement gave women similar opportunities as political agitation forced stories about women off the "women's page" and onto the news page.

Women political reporters got a leg up when Franklin D. Roosevelt was elected in 1932. Eleanor Roosevelt made news, unlike previous presidential wives, who rarely had direct contact with reporters. She held regular press conferences and was always accessible to reporters, whom she treated like professionals. Furthermore, Eleanor Roosevelt herself wrote a daily column syndicated by United Feature Syndicate, which was very popular.

There is still a corps of women reporters assigned primarily to report on the First Lady, but some of them have "graduated" to covering the President. News made by the President's wife is usually something for the social pages, and with few exceptions, newspapers still refuse to assign men to these functions. (The Washington Post's "Style" section and, occasionally, The New York Times are notable exceptions.)

In 1934 and 1935 Iona Robertson Logie surveyed 881 women for a doctoral thesis on "Careers for Women in Journalism." She found that women were consistently paid less than male colleagues and that few women held administrative or supervisory positions. Most women journalists were assigned to the usual fields of society and fashion. She found that "equality of opportunity was rare."

Of her 881 subjects, half were married, widowed, or divorced, and half single. Forty-three percent had children, and most of these women said they were distracted at work by anxiety about their children. Most hired housekeepers or nursemaids to look after their children while they were at work or arranged for a relative to baby-sit. The working wives also had primary responsibility for household chores.

A similar survey conducted today would probably produce the same answers. Working women with children still rely on baby-sitters or housekeepers and still feel guilty about it at times.

During the 1940s, 1950s, and much of the 1960s, there was little change in the status of women in journalism. There were the occasional "girl reporters" assigned to a city desk or to national affairs, a few radio and television reporters, and a few female editors, foreign correspondents, and columnists. Most women journalists continued to be found in the society, fashion, and food sections of any publication, occasionally graduating to religion or education.

It has taken many years for women to be hired in significant numbers on major papers. Looking back on the history of women in journalism, one finds recurring patterns that are surprising even today. In 1927 Micheline Keating was refused access to the press box at the World Polo championships; when she protested, she was finally allowed to sit on a folding chair just outside the all-male enclosure. In 1973 Nancy Scannell, a sportswriter for the Washington *Post,* was refused admittance to the sportswriters' snack bar during a football game. The difference was that Nancy's male colleagues stood up for her and demanded that she be let in.

Although barriers against women are breaking down every day, you may still face sexism if you enter the field of journalism. You may be told that women aren't allowed to cover a particular event. For example, Alice Bonner at the Washington *Post* was forbidden to tour a jail with a group of male reporters in 1975 because a local judge thought she might see things a woman "shouldn't see." (He was afraid she might see a man using one of the open toilets common in jails.)

Knowing that women have gone before you and have faced even greater obstacles than we face today is an inspiration. The respectability now attributed to a career in journalism is a recent phenomenon—years ago women who worked as reporters or editors were considered somehow defective and disreputable. That this attitude has largely disappeared is in part a tribute to the women who had the courage to do what hadn't been done before.

10

Job-Hunting

Looking for a job can be demoralizing and depressing. There is no way to make job-hunting pleasant, but there are ways to make it effective and relatively painless.

The first thing to do is to choose an area where you want to live. Unless you have unlimited funds to travel to job interviews, there is no point in taking on the whole country. The area you choose may be determined by the fact that you have family or friends there, it may be a place where you know someone who might be able to help you get a job, or it might simply be a place you like. You must decide which factors are most important to you.

Many people are attracted to New York or Washington because they are media centers. They are also cities where jobs are hard to get. If you have no experience, it is usually easier to find a job in a small or medium-sized town.

Once you've picked an area, consult the Yellow Pages and the *Ayer Directory* for a list of the publications or broadcast outlets in the area. Use whatever contacts you have. If your mother's best friend knows someone who might be able to give you a job, use that contact to get an introduction and perhaps an interview. You shouldn't feel shy about using these connections. No one is going to hire you unless you seem qualified for the job.

A summer job or a work-study program while you're going to school can be valuable in terms of practical experience and professional contacts when the time comes to look for a career position.

Many high schools are now developing work-study programs for their students in answer to a growing demand for "relevant" educational experiences. While many of these jobs are menial or routine, sometimes they offer the chance to learn by watching how the "professionals" work.

The federal government has a variety of youth employment programs, including some that offer jobs in the field of journalism. Sixty-four thousand of these jobs are intended for needy youths between sixteen and twenty-two, with the primary purpose of helping these young people stay in school.

Then there are summer jobs. Ten thousand jobs are available to young people who take the summer employment examination, which is generally announced in October by high school counselors or the local Civil Service Commission. Most of these jobs are routine (typing, Xeroxing). But the government also hires students for career-related jobs. For graduate students, there are between 15,000 and 18,000 positions throughout the country. Many of these jobs are learning situations, where the student has a chance to work along with professionals in the field for six months or so.

For undergraduates, there are about 7,500 work-study jobs. Work-study means going to school part time and working part time. Some programs alternate months of work with a period of study, while others provide for a half-day on campus, half-day at work arrangement.

Information on work-study jobs is generally available through your school placement office. Any school that has a bona fide co-op program, as these are called, has a responsibility to find jobs for its students. There are some work-study programs at the high school level. If your school does not have such a program, ask your local state employment service for assistance. Such work-study programs are generally intended for the student who is not going to college.

Youth Employment Opportunity director James Poole, who provided all this information, urges all students to take the initiative in finding one of these jobs. If you are interested in a journalism-related job, write directly to the public affairs or information office in the bureau that interests you. (Check the phone book under "U.S. Government" to find out which offices are located in your area.) Your letter should give your interests, your educational background, and the skills you possess, such as typing.

One reason for writing directly to different offices is that the availability of temporary positions varies from year to year. Also, if a particular office is especially impressed with your qualifications, they might make special efforts to get a temporary position assigned to their staff.

It is important to remember that hiring someone is a significant investment for any employer. It is difficult to predict whether an applicant will work out in a job. If an employer has a reference or recommendation from someone he knows and trusts, he or she is more likely to hire you.

Prepare a résumé before contacting any employer—even the government, which will also require you to fill out an application. If you have been lucky enough to get one of the government jobs mentioned earlier while you are still in school, you'll have something to put on your résumé! But any job, when you're young and haven't had much opportunity to acquire experience, should be included in your résumé at first—even working at a fast-food restaurant.

A résumé should generally be limited to one page. It should be clearly headed with your name, address, and current phone number. List your job experience next, starting with your most recent or current job. (If you have two or three or more jobs to list that are directly related to journalism, eliminate the fast-food restaurant type of experience.)

Then list your college degree(s) and honors, along with the name of your school and the year you graduated (or expect to graduate). If any of your writing has been published, include that information. If you worked on a school newspaper or broadcast facility, include that information as well.

Your résumé should also list special skills (such as a foreign language) and also include work on an unusual project in school ("helped coordinate survey on student attitudes," for example). Copies of sample résumés are usually available from placement offices. Don't send anyone a résumé without a covering letter that states what kind of a job you're looking for, summarizes your qualifications ("I have two years' experience as a general assignment reporter . . ."), and offers to provide references and copies of things you've written or tapes of a broadcast. (Some people prefer to list their references on their résumé.) Always offer to come in for an interview, and close by saying that you will follow up your letter with a phone call in a week or two.

A letter should be addressed to a specific person. Don't send in a lot of clips (published stories) with your first letter: they can get lost in the pile of applications, and one suspects that they are rarely read until an employer is actively interested in considering you. Do summarize in your letter the type and extent of writing, editing, or broadcast experience you have.

If you're looking for your first job, send letters and résumés to many different places. People have been known to apply to forty or fifty different organizations before landing a job. If you can afford to be unemployed for awhile, treat job-hunting as a job—visit every place where you might find a job, talk to the editor or personnel director, fill out applications, and leave a copy of your résumé and copies of your writing if you can.

When Gretchen Keiser graduated from college with a B.A. in philosophy and decided she wanted a job on a newspaper, she made a list of all the newspapers in her area. Then, over a period of several months, she visited thirty papers, most of them small ones, to talk to the editor in person. Eventually one newspaper needed a reporter; the editor remembered Gretchen and called to see if she was still interested. She was.

If you are looking for a job as a reporter, don't take a job as a secretary. If you have no experience at all, consider a job as a copy aide or an editorial assistant or researcher; few people are hired as reporters without any experience.

When you go to a job interview, bring copies of your work with you. Be on time, but be prepared to wait.

It's expected that you will be nervous, but you must be able to explain what kind of job you're looking for, and why you are qualified. The interviewer may ask you questions about your previous jobs, about your grades in school, about your thoughts for the future, books you've read, or anything else that strikes his or her fancy. Don't be intimidated. Just answer the questions. Don't try to impress anyone, just be yourself.

It is not proper for an interviewer to ask you whether you are pregnant, whether you plan to have children, or if you're going to get married. Interviewers can also ask insulting questions about whether or not you think you will cry on the job, or be upset if you have to work late. But these inquiries can be turned away without insulting the interviewer; flying into a feminist rage may salve your conscience, but it won't get you a job.

The same attitude can be helpful once you get the job. Women have been and perhaps always will be faced with people who assume that because they are women, they are not professionals. People you are trying to interview will call you "sweetheart" or talk to you as though you were a two-year-old; other people will raise their eyebrows at a woman who works at night.

Most women have found that if you act like a professional, you will be treated like a professional. Of course there are incidents of outright discrimination—not being allowed into a sportswriters' press box or being refused access to some area that male reporters are allowed into (like a jail or a war zone). In these cases, it is your responsibility to object, protest, fight, or do whatever you must to be able to do your job.

Sexism within the profession can be harder to fight. Women at several major news organizations, such as *The New York Times, Newsweek,* and the *Toledo*

Blade, have brought suits against their employers to force greater promotional opportunities and improved hiring practices. Employees of other news organizations have filed complaints with the Equal Employment Opportunities Commission, which makes "findings of fact" on an employer's hiring and promotion practices that may then result in a lawsuit or an agreement worked out between the management and the people who filed the complaint. Individual women have also brought suits and field complaints against different news organizations.

At the Washington *Post,* for example, a complaint that the newspaper company discriminated against women was filed with the EEOC in 1972. The complaint was filed by the Washington-Baltimore Newspaper Guild on behalf of 117 employees. One and a half years later the EEOC found that the *Post* did indeed discriminate; that women were denied equal access to higher-paying jobs in the news departments, that women reporters were given less important story assignments, and that women in the commercial departments of the newspaper were given lower salaries and restricted to certain job categories.

Although the Washington Post Company has consistently denied the allegations, since the complaint was filed there has been great improvement in the newsroom. In 1974, for example, of twenty-seven people hired, fifteen were women. There are now three women editors on the city and suburban desks, one on the national desk, and a woman reporter in the sports department.

Filing the complaint clearly spurred the company to consider its treatment of women. Technically, the EEOC findings are simply statements of fact that can provide the basis of a settlement between the *Post* and the Guild. This settlement has not yet been formalized —partly because there has already been significant improvement and partly because the Newspaper Guild has not taken the initiative in approaching the company. If a settlement is not worked out, the Guild could file a suit or the commission could seek a court-ordered settlement, which could include such things as an affirmative action plan and the awarding of back pay.

As women continue to prove their capabilities as news professionals, complicated and lengthy procedures such as an EEOC complaint will hopefully become unnecessary. But some of these actions have made it a little easier for you to get a job.

Family responsibilities should also be considered when you are looking for a job. If you decide to marry in your early twenties, your choice of a job may depend to some extent on your husband's opportunities. While it used to be standard practice that a wife allowed her husband "first choice" and then simply found what she could get after he had decided where they would live and what he would do, many young couples today are learning that giving equal emphasis to the wife's career is the better path.

Children are another factor. Statistics show that women are now choosing to have children later in their lives. Waiting until you have established yourself in a career and are earning a reasonable salary is a common choice among women today.

Deciding whether to continue working after having children can only be a personal decision. Most employers allow a woman three to six months of unpaid maternity leave, after which she may return to her old job.

Some women decide they should be at home while their children are young. Others are able to hire baby-sitters and feel that leaving their child or children in the care of another person is the best choice for them. There is no ideal choice. Baby-sitters or housekeepers can be unreliable, and leaving your children in their care makes some women feel guilty. On the other hand, staying at home for several years is frustrating for some women and can be a setback to one's career.

11

Conclusion

Journalism is a glamorous profession. It used to be glamorous and low-paying, but now it offers decent salaries (in most cases) as well as glamour.

As a result, more people than ever before want to be journalists.

Few people realize how much work is involved in putting together a responsible story or even how that story is suggested in the first place.

Let's look at one example. The local school board meets every two weeks. Material relating to the meeting is released to the press a few days before the meeting. You pick up the material and look through it—reports on pupil enrollment, petty-cash disbursements, names proposed for an advisory council, a recommendation to rescind a decision to close a particular school, and—a proposal for a completely new sex education program. Obviously, the last item is your story.

First, you read the proposed curriculum. Then, you call the supervisor whose department wrote the proposal. He is in a meeting, his secretary tells you, and will be all day. You try another curriculum specialist in the field. She's in a meeting too. You leave a message asking her to call you.

Then you start calling other school jurisdictions in the area. You want to see what sort of sex education programs they have, how they compare to the one proposed for the district you're writing about, what citizen reaction has been to the program, how long each has been in existence, and so on. You check the clips to see if anything else has been written on the subject in your newspaper. You call the head of the PTA to see if they have any reaction. Meanwhile, the supervisor who was in a meeting calls you back.

By the time you have finished researching, you have talked to seven people. You have one hour to write the story, and your editor gives you twelve inches of copy in which to explain the program, the background, the comparison to other jurisdictions, and how close the proposal is to adoption.

This story is of great interest to readers, particularly parents. No matter what you write, a lot of people won't read the whole story. They'll stop after the words "sex education" and get upset. They might call the school superintendent in anger. The school superintendent, having received angry phone calls, might call you and complain the newspaper gave the story too much attention, more than the proposal deserves. And so on.

Journalism has become an inviting profession for many because it seems to offer the chance to do something constructive in society, to bring "the truth" to the people, to right wrongs and expose corruption. This is a good motivation for deciding to be a journalist, but:

Are you prepared to spend years writing about school board meetings, crimes, or local elections?

Are you prepared to write three times as many—or more—routine stories as scandals?

Are you prepared for nasty letters and phone calls?

Are you prepared rarely to have enough time or space to do a story "right"?

The world does not need more journalists. But it does need more good journalists. There are too many mediocre newspapers and broadcast stations in this country. They produce improperly researched, poorly written, and slightly inaccurate stories that confuse and mislead the public.

A journalist has a heavy responsibility. Millions of people make decisions every day based on what they read in the newspapers. A business can become successful or be seriously undermined merely on the strength of one article. Reputations can be destroyed or improved as a result of media exposure. Theatrical productions, in some cities, live or die on the basis of what a reviewer says.

Consider this responsibility before you elect to become a journalist.

Consider also that the journalist's role is one of observing rather than participating. You listen, look, and ask questions—but you are not a part of the events that you observe. You record what other people do, not what you do yourself. You will, at times, feel you are on the outside looking in, living off the lives of other people.

Some people look to the journalist for salvation. Others wish to avoid all contact with the media. Still others are looking for free publicity. You can never take a story at face value; you must always check it out.

Opportunities will be available for you that were not there for women fifty years ago, twenty years ago, even ten years ago. These freedoms and options will allow you to concentrate on professional excellence without, one hopes, having to spend time and energy fighting for the right to have a job. You will be able to combine your career with raising a family, although it isn't easy.

The profession will demand your energy, time, thoroughness, and skill. In return, it will give you a chance to watch history being made, to observe the world and how it operates, and, perhaps, to have a sense of satisfaction at being involved in a job that society needs. You may have some adventures, travel, meet famous and interesting people and help, inform, or infuriate others.

The choice is yours.

Appendix

Schools and Departments of Journalism

ALABAMA

University of Alabama, School of Communication, University, Ala.
Samford University, Department of English and Journalism, Birmingham, Ala.
Troy State University, School of Journalism, Troy, Ala.

ALASKA

University of Alaska, Department of Journalism, Fairbanks, Alaska

ARIZONA

Arizona State University, Department of Mass Communications, Tempe, Ariz.
University of Arizona, Department of Journalism, Tucson, Ariz.
Northern Arizona University, Department of Journalism, Flagstaff, Ariz.

ARKANSAS

University of Arkansas at Fayetteville, Department of Journalism, Fayetteville, Ark.
University of Arkansas at Little Rock, Department of Journalism, Little Rock, Ark.
Arkansas State University, College of Communications, State University, Ark.
Henderson State College, Department of Journalism, Arkadelphia, Ark.

CALIFORNIA

University of California at Berkeley, School of Journalism, Berkeley, Calif.
University of California at Los Angeles, Department of Journalism, Los Angeles, Calif.
California Polytechnic State University, Journalism Department, San Luis Obispo, Calif.

California State Polytechnic University, Communication Arts, Pomona, Calif.
California State University, Center for Information and Communication Studies, Chico, Calif.
California State University, Department of Journalism, Fresno, Calif.
California State University, Department of Communications, Fullerton, Calif.
California State University, Department of Mass Communication, Hayward, Calif.
California State University, Department of Journalism, Long Beach, Calif.
California State University, Department of Journalism, Los Angeles, Calif.
California State University, Department of Journalism, Northridge, Calif.
California State University, Department of Journalism, Sacramento, Calif.
California State University, Humboldt, Department of Journalism, Arcata, Calif.
San Diego State University, Department of Journalism, San Diego, Calif.
San Francisco State University, Department of Journalism, San Francisco, Calif.
San Jose State University, Department of Journalism and Advertising, San Jose, Calif.
University of Southern California, School of Journalism, Los Angeles, Calif.
Stanford University, Department of Communication, Stanford, Calif.

COLORADO

Colorado State University, Department of Technical Journalism, Fort Collins, Colo.
University of Colorado, School of Journalism, Boulder, Colo.
University of Denver, Department of Mass Communications, Denver, Colo.
Southern Colorado State University, Department of Mass Communications, Pueblo, Colo.

CONNECTICUT

University of Bridgeport, Journalism/Communication Department, Bridgeport, Conn.
University of Connecticut, Journalism Department, Storrs, Conn.

DISTRICT OF COLUMBIA

American University, Department of Communication, Washington, D.C.
Catholic University of America, Journalism Department, Washington, D.C.
Howard University, Department of Journalism, Washington, D.C.
George Washington University, Journalism Center, Washington, D.C.

FLORIDA

Florida Southern College, Journalism Department, Lakeland, Fla.
Florida Technological University, Department of Communication, Orlando, Fla.
University of Florida, College of Journalism and Communication, Gainesville, Fla.
University of Miami, Department of Communications, Coral Gables, Fla.

University of Southern Florida, Department of Mass Communications, Tampa, Fla.

GEORGIA

University of Georgia, Grady School of Journalism, Athens, Ga.
Georgia State University, Department of Journalism, Atlanta, Ga.

HAWAII

University of Hawaii, Journalism Program, Honolulu, Hawaii

IDAHO

Idaho State University, Department of Journalism, Pocatello, Idaho
University of Idaho, School of Communication, Moscow, Idaho

ILLINOIS

Bradley University, Department of Journalism, Peoria, Ill.
University of Illinois, College of Communications, Urbana, Ill.
Northern Illinois University, Department of Journalism, DeKalb, Ill.
Northwestern University, Medill School of Journalism, Evanston, Ill.
Southern Illinois University, School of Journalism, Carbondale, Ill.
Southern Illinois University, Department of Mass Communications, Edwardsville, Ill.

INDIANA

Ball State University, Department of Journalism, Muncie, Ind.
Indiana University, School of Journalism, Bloomington, Ind.
Purdue University, Department of Communication, Lafayette, Ind.
Valparaiso University, Journalism Studies, Valparaiso, Ind.

IOWA

Drake University, School of Journalism, Des Moines, Iowa
Iowa State University, Department of Journalism and Mass Communication, Ames, Iowa
University of Iowa, School of Journalism, Iowa City, Iowa

KANSAS

Kansas State University, Department of Journalism and Mass Communications, Manhattan, Kan.
University of Kansas, School of Journalism, Lawrence, Kan.
Wichita State University, Department of Journalism, Wichita, Kan.

KENTUCKY

University of Kentucky, Department of Journalism in School of Communications, Lexington, Ky.
Morehead State University, Division of Communications, Morehead, Ky.
Murray State University, Department of Journalism, Murray, Ky.

Western Kentucky University, Department of Mass Communications, Bowling Green, Ky.

LOUISIANA

Grambling State University, Journalism Department, Grambling, La.
Louisiana State University, School of Journalism, Baton Rouge, La.
Louisiana Tech University, Journalism Department, Ruston, La.
Loyola University, Department of Journalism, New Orleans, La.
Northeast Louisiana University, Journalism Division, Monroe, La.
Northwestern State University of Louisiana, Division of Journalism, Natchitoches, La.

MAINE

University of Maine, Department of Journalism, Orono, Me.

MARYLAND

University of Maryland, College of Journalism, College Park, Md.

MASSACHUSETTS

Boston University, School of Public Communications, Boston, Mass.
University of Massachusetts, Journalistic Studies Program, Amherst, Mass.
Northeastern University, Department of Journalism, Boston, Mass.
Suffolk University, Department of Journalism, Boston, Mass.

MICHIGAN

Central Michigan University, Journalism Department, Mt. Pleasant, Mich.
University of Detroit, Communication Studies Department, Detroit, Mich.
Michigan State University, School of Journalism, East Lansing, Mich.
University of Michigan, Department of Journalism, Ann Arbor, Mich.
Wayne State University, Department of Journalism, Detroit, Mich.

MINNESOTA

Bemidji State College, Department of Mass Communications, Bemidji, Minn.
Mankato State College, Mass Communications Institute, Mankato, Minn.
University of Minnesota, School of Journalism and Mass Communications, Minneapolis, Minn.
Moorhead State College, Department of Mass Communications, Moorhead, Minn.
St. Cloud State College, Department of Mass Communications, St. Cloud, Minn.
College of St. Thomas, Department of Journalism, St. Paul, Minn.

MISSISSIPPI

Mississippi University for Women, Department of Journalism, Columbus, Miss.
University of Mississippi, Department of Journalism, University, Miss.
University of Southern Mississippi, Department of Journalism, Hattiesburg, Miss.

MISSOURI

Central Missouri State University, Department of Mass Communication, Warrensburg, Mo.
Lincoln University, Department of Journalism, Jefferson City, Mo.
University of Missouri, School of Journalism, Columbia, Mo.

MONTANA

University of Montana, School of Journalism, Missoula, Mont.

NEBRASKA

Creighton University, Department of Journalism, Omaha, Neb.
Kearney State College, Program of Journalism, Kearney, Neb.
University of Nebraska, School of Journalism, Lincoln, Neb.
University of Nebraska, Department of Journalism, Omaha, Neb.

NEVADA

University of Nevada, Department of Journalism, Reno, Nev.

NEW JERSEY

Glassboro State College, Department of Communications, Glassboro, N.J.
Rider College, Department of Communications, Trenton, N.J.
Rutgers University, Department of Human Communication, New Brunswick, N.J.

NEW MEXICO

New Mexico State University, Department of Journalism and Mass Communications, Las Cruces, N.M.
University of New Mexico, Department of Journalism, Albuquerque, N.M.

NEW YORK

Columbia University, Graduate School of Journalism, New York, N.Y.
Cornell University, Department of Communication Arts, Ithaca, N.Y.
Fordham University, Department of Communications, Bronx, N.Y.
Long Island University, Department of Journalism, Brooklyn, N.Y.
New York University, Department of Journalism and Mass Communications, New York, N.Y.
St. Bonaventure University, Department of Journalism, St. Bonaventure, N.Y.
Syracuse University, Newhouse School of Public Communications, Syracuse, N.Y.
Utica College, Department of Public Relations and Journalism, Utica, N.Y.
College of White Plains, Journalism and Communication Program, White Plains, N.Y.

NORTH CAROLINA

East Carolina University, Journalism Program, Greenville, N.C.
University of North Carolina, School of Journalism, Chapel Hill, N.C.

106

NORTH DAKOTA

North Dakota State University, Department of Communications, Fargo, N.D.
University of North Dakota, Department of Journalism, Grand Forks, N.D.

OHIO

Bowling Green State University, School of Journalism, Bowling Green, Ohio
University of Dayton, Department of Communication, Dayton, Ohio
Kent State University, School of Journalism, Kent, Ohio
Ohio State University School of Journalism, Columbus, Ohio
Ohio University, College of Communication, Athens, Ohio
Ohio Wesleyan University, Department of Journalism, Delaware, Ohio
University of Toledo, Department of Communication, Toledo, Ohio

OKLAHOMA

Central State University, Journalism Department, Edmond, Okla.
Oklahoma Baptist University, Department of Journalism, Shawnee, Okla.
Oklahoma State University, School of Journalism and Broadcasting, Stillwater, Okla.
University of Oklahoma, Herbert School of Journalism, Norman, Okla.
University of Tulsa, Department of Communications, Tulsa, Okla.

OREGON

Linfield College, Department of Communications, McMinnville, Ore.
Oregon State University, Department of Journalism, Corvallis, Ore.
University of Oregon, School of Journalism, Eugene, Ore.
Portland State University, Department of Journalism, Portland, Ore.

PENNSYLVANIA

Duquesne University, Department of Journalism, Pittsburgh, Pa.
Lehigh University, Division of Journalism, Bethlehem, Pa.
Pennsylvania State University, School of Journalism, University Park, Pa.
Point Park College, Department of Journalism and Communications, Pittsburgh, Pa.
Temple University, Department of Journalism, Philadelphia, Pa.

RHODE ISLAND

University of Rhode Island, Department of Journalism, Kingston, R.I.

SOUTH CAROLINA

University of South Carolina, College of Journalism, Columbia, S.C.

SOUTH DAKOTA

South Dakota University, Department of Journalism and Mass Communication, Brookings, S.D.
University of South Dakota, Mass Communication Sequence, Department of Communication, Vermillion, S.D.

TENNESSEE

East Tennessee State University, Department of Journalism, Johnson City, Tenn.

Memphis State University, Department of Journalism, Memphis, Tenn.

Middle Tennessee State University, Department of Mass Communications, Murfreesboro, Tenn.

University of Tennessee, College of Communications, Knoxville, Tenn.

University of Tennessee, Department of Communications, Martin, Tenn.

TEXAS

Angelo State University, Department of Journalism, San Angelo, Tex.

Baylor University, Department of Journalism, Waco, Tex.

East Texas State University, Department of Journalism and Graphic Arts, Commerce, Tex.

University of Houston, Department of Communications, Houston, Tex.

North Texas State University, Department of Journalism, Denton, Tex.

Southern Methodist University, Department of Journalism, Dallas, Tex.

Southwest Texas State University, Department of Journalism, San Marcos, Tex.

Texas A & I University, Department of Journalism, Kingsville, Tex.

University of Texas, Department of Communication, Arlington, Tex.

University of Texas, Department of Journalism, Austin, Tex.

University of Texas, Department of Mass Communication, El Paso, Tex.

Texas Christian University, Department of Journalism, Fort Worth, Tex.

Texas Technological University, Department of Mass Communication, Lubbock, Tex.

Texas Woman's University, Department of Journalism, Denton, Tex.

West Texas State University, Department of Journalism, Canyon, Tex.

UTAH

Brigham Young University, Department of Communications, Provo, Utah

Utah State University, Department of Communication, Logan, Utah

University of Utah, Department of Communication, Salt Lake City, Utah

VIRGINIA

Hampton Institute, Department of Mass Media Arts, Hampton, Va.

Virginia Commonwealth University, Department of Mass Communications, Richmond, Va.

Washington and Lee University, Lee Memorial Journalism Foundation, Lexington, Va.

WASHINGTON

Seattle University, Journalism Department, Seattle, Wash.

Washington State University, Department of Communications, Pullman, Wash.

University of Washington, School of Communications, Seattle, Wash.

Western Washington State College, Journalism Program, Bellingham, Wash.

108

WEST VIRGINIA

Bethany College, Department of Communications, Journalism, Bethany, W. Va.
Marshall University, Department of Journalism, Huntington, W. Va.
West Virginia University, School of Journalism, Morgantown, W. Va.

WISCONSIN

Marquette University, College of Journalism, Milwaukee, Wisc.
University of Wisconsin, Department of Journalism, Eau Claire, Wisc.
University of Wisconsin Extension, Department of Communication, Madison, Wisc.
University of Wisconsin, Mass Communications Department, La Crosse, Wisc.
University of Wisconsin, School of Journalism and Mass Communication, Madison, Wisc.
University of Wisconsin, Department of Agricultural Journalism, Madison, Wisc.
University of Wisconsin, Journalism Department, Milwaukee, Wisc.
University of Wisconsin, Department of Journalism, Oshkosh, Wisc.
University of Wisconsin, Department of Journalism and Mass Communications, River Falls, Wisc.

WYOMING

University of Wyoming, Department of Journalism, Laramie, Wyo.

CANADA

Carleton University, School of Journalism, Ottawa, Ont.
Ryerson Polytechnical Institute, Department of Journalism, Toronto, Ont.
University of Western Ontario, School of Journalism, London, Ont.

Bibliography

BANKS, ELIZABETH L., *Autobiography of a Newspaper Girl*. New York: Dodd, Mead, 1902.

BOUGHNER, GENEVIEVE JACKSON, *Women in Journalism*. New York: D. Appleton, 1926.

BRIER, WARREN J., and HEYN, HOWARD C., *Writing for Newspapers and News Services*. New York: Funk & Wagnalls, 1969.

BUSH, CHILTON R., *Newswriting and Reporting Public Affairs*. Philadelphia: Chilton Book, 1965 and 1970.

CHAPELLE, DICKEY, *What's a Woman Doing Here?* New York: William Morrow, 1962.

HEALY, PAUL F., *Cissy*. Garden City, N.Y.: Doubleday, 1966.

HUDSON, FREDERIC, *Journalism in the United States, 1690–1872*. Harper and Row, 1969 (written 1872–73).

LOGIE, IONA ROBERTSON, *Careers for Women in Journalism*. Scranton, Pa.: International Textbook, 1938 (published doctoral thesis).

MAYES, MARTIN, *The Development of the Press in the United States*. Richmond, Mo.: Missourian Press, 1935.

MYERS, ARTHUR, *Careers for the 70s—Journalism*. New York: Macmillan, 1971.

QUINN, SALLY, *We're Going to Make You a Star*. New York: Simon & Schuster, 1975.

ROSS, ISHBEL, *Ladies of the Press*. New York: Harper and Bros., 1936.

ST. JOHN, ADELA ROGERS, *The Honeycomb*. Garden City, N.Y.: Doubleday, 1969.

SILLER, ROBERT C., *Guide to Professional Radio and TV Newscasting*. Blue Ridge Summit, Pa.: TAB Books, 1972.

TYRRELL, ROBERT, *The Work of the Television Journalist*. New York: Hastings House, 1972.

WALKER, STANLEY, *City Editor*. New York: Frederick A. Stokes, 1934.

Pamphlets and Periodicals

Careers Unlimited, Austin Tex.: Women in Communications, Inc.

BROWN, DONALD E., *Careers in Radio and Television.* Quill and Scroll Foundation, University of Iowa.

Education for a Journalism Career, American Council on Education for Journalism.

HEATH, HARRY E., JR., *Careers in Public Relations.* Quill and Scroll Foundation, University of Iowa.

MATRIX, magazine published by Women in Communications, Inc., issues of Spring 1973 and Summer 1975.

Journalism Educator, January 1975.

A Newspaper Career and You. Princeton, N.J.: The Newspaper Fund.

Television Station Employment Practices: The Status of Minorities and Women, study by the United Church of Christ Office of Communications, New York, N.Y., December 1974.

The Voice of America, published by United States Information Agency, Washington, D.C.

Index

"A" (national) wire, 33
Advertising, 9, 69
    revenue for newspapers, 58
Agriculture publications, 53
Alternative media, 57–60
America Illustrated, 79
American Business Press, 54
American Council on Education for Journalism (A.C.E.J.), 17–19
American Indian Press Association, 36
AM radio stations, 42
Anchorpersons, 2, 40, 41
Annapolis *Evening Capitol*, 28–29
Announcers, 41, 43
Anstett, Pat, 61–62
Appearance, personal, 41–42
Ashton, Betsy, 44–46, 48, 50
Assignment editors, 27–28
Associated Press (AP), 33–35
    Teletype, 42
Ayer Directory of Publications, 54, 68, 87

"B" (local) wire, 34
Ball, Isabel Worrell, 82
Barker, Karlyn, 5, 14, 35, 83
Beat reporters, 1–2, 31, 44
"Bly, Nellie," 83
Bonner, Alice, 85–86
Boston *Globe*, 58
Boston *Post*, 82
Bredemeier, Judi, 54–57
Broadcast journalism, 40–52
    See also Radio; Television
Brochures, writing, 79
Bureaus, news, 36

Capitol, U.S., coverage, 82
Careers in the Business Press, 54
"Careers for Women in Journalism," 84
Chicago *Sun Times*, 27
Civil Service Commission, 78, 88
Civil Service exams, 79
Clips (published stories), 91
Cochrane, Elizabeth, 83

College newspapers, 5, 11–14, 16, 61, 77

College Press Service, 36

Columbia *Daily Missourian,* 12

Columbia University Graduate School of Journalism, 5, 19–22

Columnists, 60, 65, 82

Congress, U.S., coverage, 2, 82

Congressional Quarterly, 61

Contacts, story, 66–67

Content variations in news, 43–44

Contributing editors, 64, 65

Cook, Adrienne, 28–29

Cooper, Charles P., 22

Copy aides, 4, 27, 30–31, 91

Copyboys, 31

Copydesk, 30

Copy editors, 5, 27–30, 34, 38

Cornell *Daily Sun,* 12

Correspondents, 33, 36

Cronkite, Walter, 52

Daily Californian, 5, 13–14

Dawdy, Nanci Knopf, 18

D.C. Gazette, 57

Deadlines, 32–33, 45, 55, 62, 67, 77

Defense Department, 80

"Dial-A-News," 73

Dictationists, wire service, 5, 35

Directors, news, 2, 46

Discrimination, sex, 35, 85, 92–94

Dishon, Bob, 61

Dishon, Colleen, 60–61

Dummy (layout), 28–29

Economic Quarterly, 79

Editorial assistants, 91

Editorial writers, 2

Editors, 5–6, 27–30, 34, 37, 38, 55, 64, 65

Educational radio stations, 42

Education for a Journalism Career, 18

Ellerbee, Linda, 48–51

Equal Employment Opportunities Commission (EEOC), 93, 94

Esquire, 65

Everett, Cheryl, 72–74, 78

Expense records, 67

Faculties, journalism school, 17

Features and News Services, 60–62

Federal Communications Commission, 42

Feminist movement, 83–84

"Fern, Fanny," 82

"Files," newsmagazine, 36–38

Files, personal, 67

Film editors, 5–6

First Lady, coverage, 2

FM radio stations, 42

Foreign correspondents, 2

Franklin, Ann, 81

Franklin, Benjamin, 81

Freelance writers, 6, 60, 62, 64–68

General assignment reporters, 31, 44

Goddard, Mary Katherine, 81

Goddard, Sarah Updike, 81

Government agencies, 6, 78
  coverage, 55

Government jobs, 78–80

Graduate degrees
  journalism, 5, 9, 19–22
  nonjournalism, 11

Graduate students, jobs for, 88

Harvard *Crimson,* 11–13

Health, Education and Welfare, Department of, 80

Hearst, Patty, 83

Hearst, William Randolph, 83
High school journalism courses, 8
High school newspapers, 4, 5, 8
History of newswomen, 81–86
Home, working at, 61–62, 66–67
Hours, working, 3, 23–24, 54, 55, 66, 71, 76
House organs, 53
Housing and Urban Development, Department of, 80

Indiana University journalism school, 54
Internships, summer, 9, 17, 51, 79
Interviews, job, 91–92

Job-hunting, 87–95
Jobs
  competition for, 8–9, 27, 57
  preparation for, 4–5, 7–15
  types, 5–6, 27–30, 33, 36, 80
  See also Deadlines; Hours; Salaries
Johnson Space Center, 80
Journalism courses, high school, 8
Journalism departments and schools, 7–10, 16–22, 54, 61, 101–108
  newspapers, 13, 16–17
  women in, 3
Journalism Educator, 3, 16
Joy, Sally, 82
"June, Jenny," 82

Keating, Micheline, 85
Keiser, Gretchen, 21, 91
Kill fees, 67

Ladies Morning Star, 82
Ladies of the Press, 22
Lawsuits, sex discrimination, 93

Layout, newspaper, 28–29
Letters, application, 90–91
Libel, 27
Liberal arts education, 9–10
Librarians, 27, 30
Libraries, newspaper, 30
Literary Market Place, 68
Logie, Iona Robertson, 84
Los Angeles Times, 11

Magazines, 9
  government, 78–79
  special interest, 6, 53–57
  See also Newsmagazines
Magazine writing, 67–68
Majority Report, 57
Makeup editors, 27, 28
Malamud, Phyllis, 38
Managing editor, 55
Mann, Judy Luce, 4–5, 32
Maryland Journal, 81
Mathews, Jay, 12
Mathews, Linda, 11–13
Matys, Linda, 58–60
McDonald, Jean, 75–78
Michigan State journalism school, 61
"Mike fright," 46
Missouri, University of, journalism school, 16
Moore, John, 78, 80
Morgan, Midy, 82
Morgue, newspaper, 30
Mothers, working, 4, 12, 32, 50, 65–66, 74, 76–77, 84–85, 94–95

National Commission on Accrediting, 17
National Observer, 62
National Scholastic Press Association, 8

Newell, William, 82
Newport Mercury, 81
Newscasters, 43, 46
Newsletters, 70, 72, 75
Newsmagazines, 6, 25, 36–38
Newspaper Career and You, 10, 19
Newspaper Fund, The, 8–10, 19
Newspaper Guild, 93, 94
Newspapers, 1–2, 9, 26–33
  alternative, 57–60
  daily, 6, 23–33
  local, 4, 15, 28–29
  school. *See* College newspapers;
    High school newspapers; Jour-
    nalism departments and schools
  special interest, 57
  urban, 15, 28–29
  weekly, 6, 26, 32, 58
Newspaper writing, 25–26, 43–44
News reporting, variations, 25–26,
  34, 43–44, 58
Newsweek, 36–38, 92
Newsworks, 57
New York *Daily News,* 25–26
New York *Herald,* 82
New York *Post,* 25–26
New York *Sun,* 82
New York Times, The, 25–26, 56,
  82, 84, 92
New York *Tribune,* 82
New York *World,* 83

Oddbody, Ann, 82

Pamphlets, 79
Peterson, Dr. Paul, 8
Photographers, 27
Pittsburgh Saturday Visiter, 82
Politello, Dario, 12
Poole, James, 89
Presidents, U.S. coverage, 2, 31

Press conferences, 70, 75
Press releases, 70, 72, 73, 75
  high school, 8
Press secretaries, 75–78
Pressures in journalism, 3–4
Problems of Communism, 79
Producers, news, 2, 6, 43, 46
Professional Administrative Career
  Examination, 80
Providence Gazette, 81
Public information, 2, 71–74
  offices, 79
  specialists, 6
Public relations, 9, 67–71
  courses, 70
  executives, 6
  noncommercial, 71

Queries, story-idea, 66, 67
Quotations, reporting, 25–26

Rabin, Jeffrey, 13–14
Radio, 2
  college courses, 16
  newsprograms, 42, 44–46
  newswriting, 43–44
  stations, 6, 9, 42
Reader's Digest, 68
Religious publications, 53–54
Reporters, 38–39
  newsmagazine, 36–37
  newspaper, 1–2, 23–24, 27, 31,
    37, 50, 51
  radio, 40–41, 44–46
  syndicate, 61–62
  television, 2, 40–43, 47–51
  wire service, 5
  women, numbers of, 2–3
Reports, government, 79
Research assistants, 27, 30
Researchers, 37, 91

Resumés, 90–91
Richman, Phyllis, 65–68
Roosevelt, Eleanor, 84
Roosevelt, Franklin D., 84
Ross, Ishbel, 22

St. John, Adela Rogers, 83
St. Petersburg *Times,* 28–29
Salaries or fees, 3, 35, 45, 48, 59, 64–65, 68, 71, 74, 78, 80, 93
Scannell, Nancy, 85
Simpson, Peg, 34–35
"Sob sisters," 83
Specialization, 11, 54, 65, 67
Sportswriters, 2, 85
Stanford University newspaper, 77
Stein, M.L., 10
Stringers, 33, 60, 61, 64
"Stunt journalism," 83
Style variations, 25–26, 34, 58, 67–68
Submissions, multiple, 67
Suffrage movement, 83
Summer jobs, 7, 17, 51, 79, 88
Supreme Court coverage, 2, 11
Swisshelm, Jane, 82
Syndicates, 60–63, 84

"Talking heads," 47
Television, 2
    closed circuit, 8
    college courses, 16
    news programs, 42–43, 46–52
    news writing, 43–44
    stations, 9, 42
Time, 36, 37
Time pressures, 41
    See also Deadlines
Toledo Blade, 92–93
Trade journals, 54–57
TravelAge East, 55, 56

TravelAge Mid-America, 55, 56
TravelAge West, 55, 56
Travel Management Daily, 55, 56
Travel Management Newsletter, 55
TravelScene, 55, 56
Trenton Times, 27, 29

Undergraduate journalism schools, 16–19
Undergraduates, jobs for, 89
United Feature Syndicate, 84
United Press International (UPI), 5, 33–35
    Teletype, 42
United States Information Agency, 78–79
U.S. News and World Report, 36

Valley Advocate, 58–60
"Visuals," 47
Voice, impression of, 42, 52
Voice of America, 79
Volunteer work, 51, 59, 77

Wall Street coverage, 2
Wall Street Journal, 56
Walters, Barbara, 40
Washingtonian magazine, 62, 65
Washington *Post,* 4–5, 27, 83, 85, 93
    "Style," 84
    Sunday magazine, 65
Waters, Lyssa, 19–22
White House
    coverage, 2, 31
    jobs, 80
Wire services, 6, 9, 25, 33–36
    See also Associated Press; United Press International
Wives, working, 4, 56, 76–77, 94
    See also Mothers, working

Woman, 82
Women, numbers in journalism,
   2–3, 71
Women's pages, 2, 82–83, 84–85
Work-study programs, 88, 89
Writers
   broadcast news, 43–44
   magazine, 64–68

newsmagazine, 36–38
   See also Reporters
Writer's Market, 68
Writer's Yearbook, 68

Youth Employment Opportunity,
   89
   programs, 88–89

About the Author

Megan Rosenfeld has worked for the Washington *Post* since Dec., 1971, starting as a news aide in their *Style* section. A graduate of Antioch College, she is now assigned to the Virginia desk of the *Post*. As a general assignment reporter, she writes several articles a week on a variety of subjects, and free-lance articles when she can find the time. This is her first book.